SOUTH WEST
COAST PATH

SOUTH WEST COAST PATH

Exmouth to Poole

Roland Tarr

Photographs by Mike Williams
General editor Michael Allaby

AURUM PRESS

COUNTRYSIDE COMMISSION · ORDNANCE SURVEY

ACKNOWLEDGEMENTS

My thanks to the following organisations and people for help and advice: the
Devon and Wessex Regional Offices of the National Trust and the National
Trust wardens; the planning and highways departments of Devon and Dorset
County Councils; the Dorset and East Devon Heritage Coast Services; English
Nature local offices; Exmouth Tourist Information Centre; Jo Draper for
checking the Dorset historical bits; Sarah Welton for the article on marine
wildlife; Norman Barns for helping me find my way through the Axmouth–
Lyme Regis Undercliffs.

Roland Tarr was born in West Somerset and has close family ties with Dorset,
where for 14 years he was Heritage Coast Officer.

This edition first published 1989 by Aurum Press Ltd in association
with the Countryside Commission and the Ordnance Survey
Reprinted 1990
Revised edition published 1996. Updated 1999
Text copyright © 1989, 1996, 1999 by Aurum Press Ltd, the Countryside
Commission and the Ordnance Survey
Maps Crown copyright © 1989, 1996, 1999 by the Ordnance Survey
Photographs copyright © 1989 by the Countryside Commission

Ordnance Survey, Pathfinder and Travelmaster are registered trademarks
and the OS symbol, Explorer and Outdoor Leisure are trade marks of Ordnance
Survey, the national mapping agency of Great Britain.

A Catalogue Record for this book is available from the British Library
ISBN 1 85410 389 X

Book design by Robert Updegraff
Cover photograph: Worbarrow Bay from Gad Cliff
Title page photograph: Swyre Head near Lulworth Cove

Typeset by Wyvern 21 Ltd, Bristol
Printed and bound in Italy by Printers Srl, Trento

CONTENTS

Circular walks appear on pages 43, 44, 66, 114, 128, 146 and 147

How to use this guide

The 613-mile (987-kilometre) South West Coast Path is covered by four national trail guides. Each guide describes a section of the path between major estuaries. This book describes the Path from Exmouth to Poole, 99 miles (160 kilometres).

This guide is in three parts:

• The introduction, historical background to the area and advice for walkers.

• The Path itself, described in eleven chapters, with maps opposite each route description. This part of the guide also includes information on places of interest as well as a number of related short walks, either starting from the Path itself or at an inland car park. Key sites are numbered both in the text and on the maps to make it easier to follow the route description.

• The last part includes useful information such as local transport, accommodation, organisations involved with the Path and further reading.

The maps have been prepared by the Ordnance Survey for this trail guide using 1:25 000 Pathfinder®, Explorer™ or Outdoor Leisure™ maps as a base. The line of the Coast Path is shown in yellow, with the status of each section of the Path – footpath or bridleway for example – shown in green underneath (see key on inside front cover). These rights of way markings also indicate the precise alignment of the Path, which walkers should follow. In some cases, the yellow line on these maps may show a route which is different from that shown on older maps; walkers are recommended to follow the yellow route in this guide, which will be the route that is waymarked with the distinctive acorn symbol 🌰 used for all national trails. Any parts of the Path that may be difficult to follow on the ground are clearly highlighted in the route description. *Black arrows (*→*) at the edge of the maps indicate the start point.* Should there have been a need to alter the route since publication of this guide, for any reason, walkers are advised to follow any waymarks or signs which have been put up on site to indicate this. Since the Coast Path passes through or near army firing ranges, walkers are asked to pay particular attention to the advice in these chapters. Alternative routes around the Lulworth Ranges are shown should you be unable to continue your journey along the Coast Path because firing is taking place.

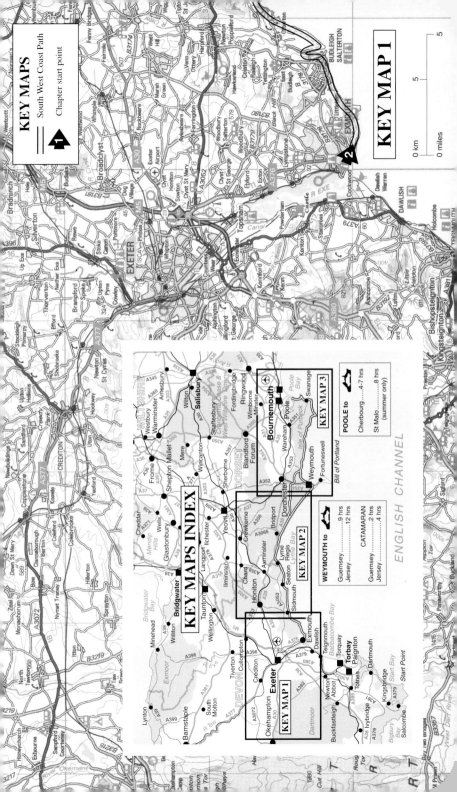

KEY MAPS

South West Coast Path

▲1 Chapter start point

KEY MAP 1

0 km   5   5
0 miles   5   5

KEY MAPS INDEX

KEY MAP 3

POOLE to
Cherbourg .... 4–7 hrs
St Malo .... 8 hrs
(summer only)

KEY MAP 2

WEYMOUTH to
Guernsey .... 9 hrs
Jersey .... 12 hrs

CATAMARAN
Guernsey .... 2 hrs
Jersey .... 4 hrs

KEY MAP 1

ENGLISH CHANNEL

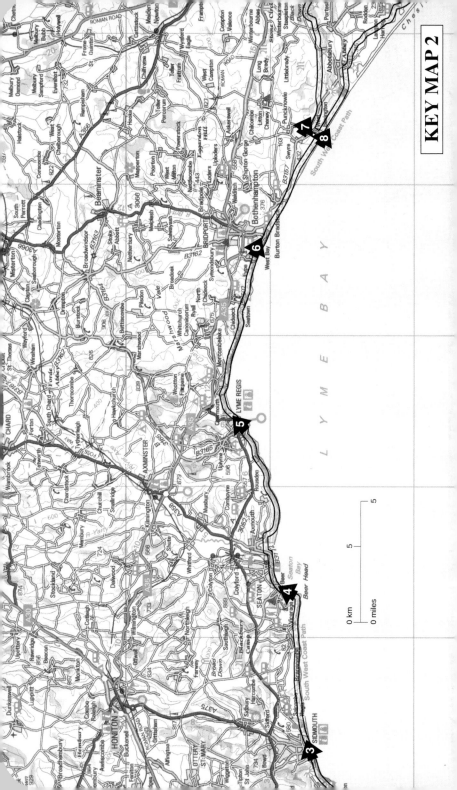

KEY MAP 2

KEY MAP 3

Distance checklist

This list will assist you in calculating the distances between places on the Path where you may be planning to stay overnight, or in checking your progress along the way.

location on coastal route	approx. distance from previous location	
	miles	km
Exmouth	0	0
Budleigh Salterton	4.2	6.8
Sidmouth	7.0	11.3
Beer	8.2	13.2
Axe Bridge (for Axmouth) [Axe Bridge–Axmouth 0.9 miles/1.5 km]	1.9	3.1
Lyme Regis	6.7	10.8
Charmouth	2.2	3.5
Seatown (for Chideock) [Seatown–Chideock 0.8 miles/1.3 km]	4.1	6.6
West Bay (for Bridport YHA) [West Bay–Bridport YHA 1.6 miles/2.6 km]	3.1	5.0
West Bexington	5.6	9.0
Abbotsbury	3.6	5.8
Langton Herring (1 mile/1.6 km off route)	5.1	8.2
Weymouth (Clock Tower)	10.2	16.4
Osmington Mills	4.5	7.2
Lulworth Cove	7.4	11.9
Kimmeridge (0.7 mile/1.1 km off route)	7.4	11.9
Worth Matravers (0.9 mile/1.5 km off route)	8.7	14.0
Langton Matravers (1.2 miles/1.9 km off route)	3.7	6.0
Swanage	5.6	9.0
Studland	4.5	7.2
Poole (Sandbanks ferry)	3.0	4.8

location on inland route		
West Bexington	0	0
Litton Cheney YHA (2.7 miles/4.3 km off route)	4.9	7.9
Martinstown (1.6 miles/2.6 km off route)	10.3	16.6
Upwey (0.4 mile/0.6 km off route)	4.6	7.4
Osmington	6.8	10.9
Osmington Mills	1.2	1.9

PREFACE

The South West Coast Path follows the spectacular fringe of one of Britain's most popular coastal holiday areas from Minehead in Somerset, through Devon and Cornwall to Poole in Dorset. The section covered in this book, from Exmouth to Poole, skirts Lyme Bay and Chesil Beach eventually taking the walker around the beautiful Isle of Purbeck coast to the end of the path in Poole.

The variety of coastal scenery on this section of the Path is remarkable, from the undulating cliffs of Lyme Bay to the spectacular bank of Chesil Beach and the white chalky cliffs of Purbeck. It is a relatively unspoilt and quiet stretch of coastline which is deceptively challenging to walkers. Circular walks inland make the path attractive to day visitors as well as to the seasoned long-distance walker.

Local Authorities work with organisations such as the National Trust to maintain the path using Countryside Commission funding. The exposed nature of the path and its popularity make this a major task in some areas. The path is waymarked with a distinctive acorn symbol which signals that you are on the right route.

I hope you will enjoy using this book during many hours of walking on this delightful stretch of England's coastline.

Richard Simmonds
Chairman
Countryside Commission

PART ONE

INTRODUCTION

The landscape along the Coast Path

Contrasts and variety of landscape are the great assets of this path. The cliffs vary from the red sandstone of East Devon to the black layers of Blue Lias around Lyme Regis and the Kimmeridge clays, jet black when wet. The light grey vertical limestone of the cliffs between Worth Matravers and Swanage contrasts subtly with the dazzling white chalk cliffs of Ballard Down, overlooking Poole Harbour. Each cove has its own distinctive character. Every nook and cranny has its true stories of shipwrecks and smuggling.

The discovery of ample coal supplies and steam power led to manufactured goods being produced more cheaply in the industrial north and to the demise of the great weaving and spinning trades associated with wool production which thrived for centuries in the south of England.

Nevertheless, the wealth associated with the heyday of the southern wool trade has left us great monuments of those times in the form of stately homes, manor houses and medieval churches which represent some of the finest rural architecture to be found anywhere in Europe. Many of these are within sight or walking distance of the South West Coast Path. Wildlife, too, is in abundance.

Even in the depths of winter walking this route can be a beautiful experience. With suitable clothing one can keep warm and dry, and often the views into the distance, to both ends of Lyme Bay and to the Isle of Wight, can be stunningly clear.

Because the water in the estuaries and lagoons along this coast rarely, if ever, freezes many species of wildfowl migrate from the far northern wastes of Scandinavia and Europe to spend the winter somewhere a little warmer.

Time spent with good binoculars on any of these estuaries gives great pleasure both to the newcomer making fresh discoveries and to the experienced bird watcher, who will be able to identify a vast range of birds, and who will almost certainly be surprised by the odd rarities which stray here from time to time.

The estuaries of the Exe, the Otter, the Axe, the Lagoon of the Fleet, the Royal Society for the Protection of Birds reserves at Radipole and Lodmoor and, largest of all, Poole Harbour with its 100 miles of shoreline would alone make an unforgettable holiday for anyone who walked this route during the winter.

The flora varies with the changing soils. Perhaps the most spectacular period is in the spring and early summer. Every wood and many of the meadows will be full of bluebells and primroses. Red campion, stitchwort, scarlet pimpernel and orchids will crop up regularly right beside the path. In Dorset, chalk and limestone downland plants thrive on grassy cliff tops, sometimes making a carpet of wild thyme, milkwort, eyebright, and ladies' bedstraw – so called because it was put into old straw to make it seem fresh in the stable sleeping quarters of medieval hostelries.

In more remote areas you are likely to come across roe deer, foxes and badgers. At Kimmeridge Bay you can explore the colourful marine wildlife.

Meanwhile the heathland reserves at Studland form a complete contrast to everything which has been seen before to the west. Here a guided walk with the warden might reveal all six British reptiles – the smooth snake, grass snake, adder, slow worm, common lizard and the surprisingly large and colourful sand lizard, which few people on our island have ever seen.

Sandy beaches are few and far between. Exmouth, Weymouth, Swanage and Studland are the only ones of any size. Nevertheless, the other, shingle beaches are excellent for swimming and sunbathing in the summer and early autumn.

Archaeological remains will be seen every day, with their traces of how people lived in this area during the last 7,000 years. All along the route there are ancient hill forts and burial mounds, but the most remarkable concentration is found on the South Dorset Ridgeway, referred to as the inland route of the Dorset Coast Path, where it passes to the north of Weymouth.

For full enjoyment of this route one needs fine clear days when the horizon can be seen clearly out to sea, the Isle of Portland set magnificently in clear blue waters to the south, and virtually all the hills of Dorset in the distance to the north, crowned with yet more hill forts and evidence of our past. On such fine days the South Dorset Ridgeway can be one of the most inspiring walks, although on other occasions you may wonder why you are wandering around among the farmers' fields.

Under Enterprise Neptune (see page 35) the National Trust has bought a considerable part of this coastline. In Dorset, for example, the Trust owns one-third of the land through which the Coast Path passes. Along this stretch you will see small valleys where traditional farming is still carried out, hedgerows are preserved and wildlife thrives, often as a result of careful management by the National Trust in conjunction with local farmers.

The Path passes by nationally famous landmarks such as Ladram Bay, The Cobb at Lyme Regis, Black Ven and Golden Cap. It gives views of the impressive sweep of the Chesil Bank (or Beach as it is on the maps) and of the Isle of Portland, source of the stone for many buildings in London.

A little further east come Durdle Door and Lulworth Cove, famous examples of folding rocks and the erosive properties of the sea. From the eastern side of Lulworth Cove to the western side of Kimmeridge Bay stretch the once much disputed Lulworth army ranges, described as one of the last great wildernesses on the south coast of England and largely unaffected by modern farming practices. The ranges have produced a landscape totally different from any other along the Path, so it is worth timing your walk so you can include this section in your journey. The ranges are open most weekends and school holidays; check by telephoning Bindon Abbey (01929) 462721.

Kimmeridge Bay, with its fascinating marine wildlife and industrial history, is followed by the Purbeck stone mines, source of the famous Purbeck marble which adorns many of the cathedrals of Europe.

Poole Harbour, one of the great boating centres of the south coast of England, is beautiful in its own right as well as being a protected wildlife area of international importance.

The unforgettable part of the experience of walking this path will be the ever-changing scenery. Every mile or two a completely different view will present itself and each of these views will be remembered with pleasure for many years to come.

Planning your walk

Each of the chapters describes one easy day's walking, an average of ten to twelve miles (16 to 19 km) assuming that the walker will wish to spend time looking at some of the wildlife, the geology, the architecture of the small village churches or

Charmouth, one of Dorset's coastal resorts.

some of the other fascinating things which may catch the eye along this coast. Many people allow about ten days to walk from Exmouth to Poole. Plan to average one to two miles (1.5 to 3 km) per hour to allow time to explore and take the difficult bits at a leisurely pace.

What time of year is best? Autumn and winter are without a doubt the most dramatic times to walk on this coast. You will see the East Devon and Dorset coasts at their wildest and most majestic, and often have the coast to yourself. You will see many colourful species of wintering birds which migrate to escape the rigours of the arctic regions.

Marine life and its industrial past are the attractions of Kimmeridge Bay.

Spring is good for flowers and, taking care to avoid public holidays, the cliffs will be relatively uncrowded, particularly on weekdays. In addition to bird and flower books, try to take some of the new-style miniature binoculars which you can carry in your pocket. These will save weight and time when you need to get them out quickly.

Early summer is also a good time for the wild flowers. Midsummer and autumn can be very peaceful and often warm, but August can be overcrowded.

Equipment

This is one of the mildest and driest parts of the United Kingdom. In winter, when the most beautiful views will be obtained, you should, of course, allow for the possibility of freezing weather. If you can afford it, a top-grade down jacket with a hood, which can be reduced to a small size when packed tightly into a purpose-made bag, can guarantee warmth whatever the conditions.

On those days when it does rain, good-quality waterproofs will make an enormous difference to the enjoyment of your walking. Plastic waterproofs, which you may use for short excursions near home, can be extremely sweaty and uncomfortable when you are fighting your way from sea level to 500 feet (150 metres) during a sudden downpour, or, worse still, when it decides to rain all day.

Some form of breathable waterproof gear is much better. There are several makes on sale in good camping shops. At first sight such gear may appear expensive, but having bought it you will never again worry about a rainy day.

Some of the walks could be done in plimsolls during a dry period, but leather walking shoes with commando-style grips, or mountain boots, are better. They will prevent you from slipping on the steep slopes, making your walk easier as well as safer. Always 'run them in' for three or four days, even if it means wearing them around the house. This will save blisters and discomfort at the beginning of your walking holiday.

As most of the directions in this guide use 'north, south, east, west' terminology you may find a compass useful.

Camping

For camping, a maximum of a 75-litre rucksack during the winter and a 50-litre rucksack during the summer is recommended. The maximum weight including tent, sleeping bag, all spare clothing and cameras need not exceed 28 pounds (13 kilograms). It is amazing how little you need to exist for days on end without carrying vast weights on your back.

There are many camp sites along the way but, if it is not possible to reach one, farmers along the route are often happy to give permission to *bona fide* walkers.

Youth hostels and bed and breakfast

If you are youth hostelling or staying in bed and breakfast accommodation, all you will need is warm gear for cold days, waterproofs, a camera, this guide, and good bird and flower guides.

Booking is absolutely essential during school holiday periods and summer weekends, but during the rest of the year walking can be much more relaxed and flexible if you stay wherever the fancy takes you each night.

For bed and breakfast in the villages it is best to enquire at the village shop, post office or pub. This is a long established holiday area and you should have few problems.

Safety precautions

Sensible walkers need have little to worry about on safety grounds. There are, however, a few accidents each year. None of the cliffs of this coast is stable at any time.

Rock falls often consist of many thousands of tons of rock. People who do not keep well away from the base of higher cliffs, especially when spending a large part of one day in the same place, are at particular risk.

The other cause of accidents is slipping inadvertently on steep ground or tripping over, often as a result of looking at the view instead of the path. Occasionally broken bones or lesions which need stitches are the result, so a whistle may be useful to attract attention if you are alone, as well as a first-aid kit. Swimming is generally safe in the coves but, on more exposed parts of the coast, watch the water carefully for currents and observe any warning signs.

Walking along the beach is usually very hard work. If you do so, take great care not to be cut off by a rising tide, by consulting local tide tables beforehand. If no tide tables are displayed locally, or if you are planning your walk from a distance, the coastguards will be glad to give you the tide times, and their telephone number will be found in the local telephone directory.

PART TWO

SOUTH WEST COAST PATH
Exmouth to Poole

1 Crossing the Exe

If you are walking the South Devon section of the Path in summer and need to cross the Exe, you can catch the Starcross Ferry which runs an hourly service, seven days a week, from May to October. It leaves Starcross from 10 a.m. to 4 p.m. on the hour daily with an additional last ferry at 5 p.m., May to October, 5.45 p.m. in July and August. It leaves Exmouth for Starcross from 10.30 a.m. to 4.30 p.m. on the half hour, with an additional last ferry at 5.30 p.m. May to October, 6.15 p.m. in July and August. The ferry is reached through Starcross Station **1**.

Near the station is the site of Brunel's Atmospheric Pumping Station, a relic of one of the great experiments of 19th century industrial enterprise. The general idea was literally to vacuum trains along the new line from Exeter to Newton Abbot. The railway actually carried passengers for a whole year in 1847 and speeds of nearly 70 m.p.h. (112 km/h.) were reported before financial problems forced the experiment to cease.

If you are in a hurry and the Starcross Ferry is not running at the time, catch a train into Exeter from Dawlish or Dawlish Warren and then back to Exmouth, using the regular services on both sides of the estuary.

At the time of writing there is an hourly service on weekdays between Dawlish and Exeter St David's **4**. At weekends it is a two-hourly service. Between Exeter St David's and Exmouth there is a half-hourly service on weekdays, a little less frequently on Sundays.

If going from Exmouth to Dawlish it would be worth going to the moorings at the quay at the mouth of the Exe **8** and hailing the 'Water Taxi Service'. At the time of writing, this was operating from 8 a.m. to 6 p.m. from April to the end of October, on request in person from the Exmouth side, or by hailing from the Dawlish Warren side, or by phoning the night before (01392) 873409.

Perhaps the most attractive way to cross the Exe, and certainly the most interesting, is to walk the whole way from Dawlish Warren to Topsham. This is about 6 miles (10 km) of flat walking, half of which is on country lanes. You may prefer to avoid 2 miles (3 km) of walking on roads by catching the train to Starcross **1**.

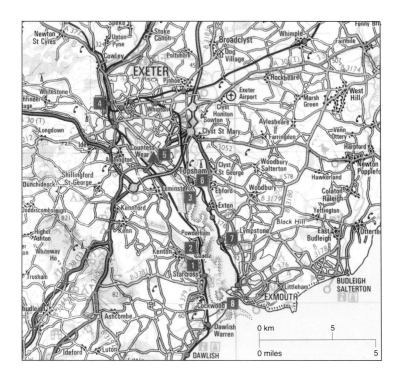

Then you can visit the historic Powderham Church **2**, enjoy views across the Exe, and possibly see fishermen at work seining. This ancient method of fishing for salmon involves two small boats with a long narrow net stretched between them. Gradually the net is brought round in a circle to enclose a pond-sized stretch of river and, with luck, a large salmon is caught.

You will have time to inspect the ancient Exeter Canal which was started in 1564, and Topsham is well worth a visit.

Follow the roads along the western side of the River Exe through Starcross and past Powderham Castle. On reaching Powderham Church **2** on a sharp corner, continue north along a track, cross the railway after 300 yards, and follow the dyke northwards for 1½ miles (2 km). You will eventually come to the seaward end of the Exeter Canal.

The Turf Inn stands by the lockside and sometimes ancient barges are moored there.

The walk north along the west towpath to Topsham takes only half an hour and is very attractive. At Topsham there is a bridge over the canal and a ferry **3** across the Exe which runs every day except Tuesdays April–September. This can be hailed during the following times: 11 a.m. to 5.30 p.m. May–September inclusive, and at weekends only 11 a.m.–5.30 p.m. October–April, subject to tides and weather. Lunch break is normally 1 p.m. to 2 p.m., but may be varied to allow for tides.

The town lies on a tongue of land between the Exe and the Clyst. If you walk south from the ferry you will come to the Strand, with beautiful houses built in the Dutch style by merchants who traded with The Netherlands in past centuries. The houses still have their Dutch-style private courtyards and enclosed gardens. Among these merchants' houses is the museum, Holman House (number 25), open 2 p.m.–5 p.m. Mondays, Wednesdays and Saturdays and most Sundays from June to September, and well worth a visit.

You can continue to the end of the Strand along a footpath/quay, then turn left through the country lanes and cross the railway bridge to get to the ancient bridge crossing the Clyst **6** and the riverside pub. Turn left and you will come to Topsham Station in a couple of minutes. From Topsham to Exmouth there is a half-hourly train service offering good views of the estuary.

A further route via Countess Wear would take you to Starcross and Powderham Church **2**, and along the banks of the Exe to the Turf Inn, following the route just described. You then follow the Exeter Canal all the way to Countess Wear, where you can stay overnight in the youth hostel **5**.

A mile or so before you reach Countess Wear you pass under the M5 motorway and when you get to the A38 turn right by the swing bridge, cross the old bridge over the Exe and take the first turning on the left by the café. The youth hostel **5** is a short way down this road.

To return to the Coast Path at Exmouth you can walk along a riverside public footpath to Topsham from Countess Wear. However, this involves scrambling along the muddy banks of the estuary and the path is flooded at high tide.

I would therefore advise walking back along the Exeter Canal, from the swing bridge at Countess Wear to Topsham, and crossing the Exe by the ferry there **3** (see running times on page 159). From Topsham you can catch the half-hourly train service to Exmouth.

Walking the road between Topsham and Lympstone is not recommended, but the railside public footpath Lympstone to Exmouth is narrow but passable.

The Exe Estuary – trade, towns and villages

This area is steeped in history for which much of the evidence can still be seen today. This makes it fascinating to explore.

Exeter and Countess Wear

We know that the Romans regarded Exeter as being of strategic importance since it was served by the Foss Way, and any coastal towns or villages with sea access would have been important at the time both for defence and trade.

If you have followed the paths described above to Countess Wear, with its beautiful old bridge and weir across the Exe, you may already have come across the story of the Countess.

She was the Countess of Devonshire, Isabella de Fortibus, and held considerable power, but the City of Exeter, like most medieval cities, was keen to claim its independence. In 1284 the Countess Isabella sent her bailiff to Exeter fish market to collect tithes, which the mayor refused to pay.

The story goes that in retaliation she commanded the construction of the weir which bears her name in order, she said, to supply water power to a mill. The weir then cut the city off from the sea completely. Exeter could no longer function as a port. The city fought back and won the legal action but the weir is still there to the present day.

Exeter had been a major outlet for the hinterland, with ships setting sail to all parts of the known world. The construction of the weir ensured that Topsham now became the major outlet and for two and a half centuries this state of affairs worked much to the benefit of the merchants of Topsham, causing a sharp decline in the wool trade of Exeter.

Then, in the 16th century, Exeter decided to fight back by constructing a canal beside the Exe Estuary just below Topsham, thus bypassing the weir. This was extended in subsequent centuries and Exeter once again became a thriving port. A visit to the Exeter Maritime Museum is worthwhile if you wish to know more about all this, and a map in the Turf Inn shows the different periods of construction.

Topsham

Topsham 6 lies at the confluence of the River Clyst, which lends its name to a number of Devon villages, and the Exe. A fine stone bridge crosses the Clyst by a weir and the ancient and traditional Bridge Inn. Topsham may be the original Roman port referred to in this area. This is not certain, but we do know that a settlement existed by the time of Domesday. After the construction of the weir on the Exe it became not only an important port but also a shipbuilding centre.

This trade still provides employment in Topsham, as you will observe as you walk along the river edge, and activity was particularly lively in the 19th century when a spur was built from the railway station to the docks. As you walk around Topsham you can still see some of the store houses and the Dutch gabled buildings along the Strand. To find out more about the Dutch connection visit the fascinating museum at number 25.

Lympstone

If, in crossing the estuary by one of the methods described above, you get out of the train at Lympstone 7 and follow the rather narrow footpath alongside the estuary to Exmouth, you will be able to enjoy visiting this attractive village. There are Georgian houses and thatched cottages, and in former centuries boats were also constructed here. At the end of the 19th century a fleet of 100 fishing vessels operated from the village.

Exmouth

Exmouth is now a busy seaside resort with a large beach offering a range of holiday activities. In the past, like other coastal ports, Exmouth was expected to send ships in times of conflict to help defend the nation. From Viking times onwards there are frequent stories of the town being sacked by foreign powers as well as by pirates, but until the 18th century it remained a small town centred on the port.

At the very beginning of the fashion for seaside resorts, sea-water baths were constructed and it became fashionable to own a large house with its own stables and a view of the sea. Assembly rooms were built and the town has now had nearly 300 years of providing for visitors. Many famous people took up residence in the town, including Lady Nelson and Lady Byron. This is reflected in a number of fine buildings which can still be seen. Exmouth has a museum, which includes a display on the Exe Estuary's maritime and natural history. It is at Shepherd's Walk, off Exeter Road near the town centre shopping precinct.

Topsham merchants closely connected with The Netherlands built their houses in the Dutch style.

2 Exmouth to Sidmouth

via Budleigh Salterton
11¼ miles (18 km)

Setting out from Exmouth, make for the cliffs at the eastern end of the Esplanade. At the far side of The Maer, a recreation ground opposite the sandy beach, the roads fork.

In the fork there is a café, toilets and car park. Go to the landward side of this car park and turn into Foxholes Hill. As the road bears inland the Coast Path forks right off it and stays on the cliff, from the top of which there are views across the River Exe to Starcross, the cliffs of Dawlish Warren and beyond.

Going east, the path from Exmouth to Budleigh Salterton is on the cliff top throughout its length. There is a Royal Marines firing range 2 miles (3 km) east of Exmouth, next to a large caravan site at Sandy Bay keep along the cliff top until you come

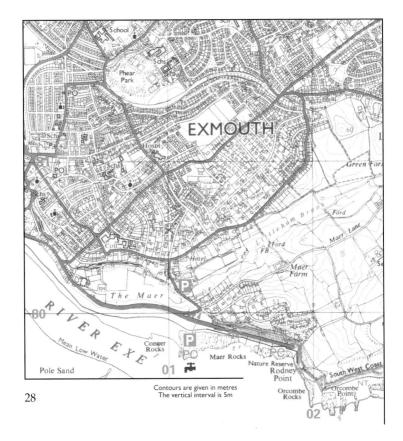

Contours are given in metres
The vertical interval is 5m

to the firing range fence, then turn left and follow the fence, keeping the firing range on the seaward side. Shortly after passing the firing range entrance on your right, turn left again and cross a large open meadow which is part of the caravan site to rejoin the cliff top as it rises.

Just east of Exmouth there are access points to sandy beaches at Orcombe Rocks (National Trust) and at Sandy Bay. Here there are telephones and toilets, a café and a bar which are open during the holiday season. Regular (no. 5) bus services run to Exmouth from early May until early September.

To the east of the caravan site the path climbs, dropping only briefly through a tiny valley before rising to the heights of 'The Floors'.

At West Down Beacon there is a trig point beside the path and one or two seats. From this point there is a fairly gentle descent keeping to the cliff top alongside the East Devon Golf Club down to the Marine Parade at Budleigh Salterton.

This quiet resort with Georgian, Victorian and Edwardian

Contours are given in metres
The vertical interval is 5m

houses fronting the sea is pleasant and relaxing. Shops and pubs should be able to supply all your needs and the Tourist Information Centre can help with accommodation. If you find it closed, a list of accommodation addresses can be found on the door.

Now follow the road and then the path along the crest of the beach. When you come into sight of the Otter estuary go to the far corner of the large car park beside it and then walk three-quarters of a mile north beside the River Otter on a dyke built by Napoleonic prisoners of war. Cross the Otter, go straight ahead along the road for 100 yards (90 metres) and then turn right along the path just inside the next field and return to the sea along the bank opposite. Note the nature reserve of the Devon Wildlife Trust. There is a hide constructed by the East Devon Heritage Coast Service.

Continue along the cliff top towards Ladram Bay. Just before Ladram the path crosses a stile and cuts across the next field, making for a gap at the eastern end and a footbridge. It continues along the landward side of the next field until it comes to the small lane. This leads down to Ladram Bay with its shingle beach, red sandstone stacks and small caves.

Contours are given in metres
The vertical interval is 5m

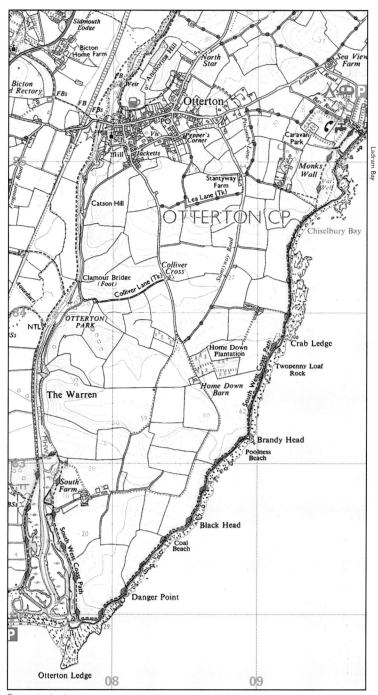

Ladram Bay

During the summer season all facilities are present at the Bay including a telephone and a tea shop for Devon cream teas. Going eastward, the path stays on top of the cliff until it enters a plantation in which lies the Iron Age hill fort of High Peak. There is now a Marine Awareness Centre located at the top of the slipway, across the Coast Path. This was opened by The Heritage Coast Service in 1997, to give visitors information on the marine environment. It is open Sundays to Thursdays, Easter to September.

The path then follows the well-defined tracks through the woods just inland of High Peak, and continues along the cliff top to Peak Hill. The Coast Path to the east goes down through the woods, branching right at the junction before turning inland along a garden fence. Steps lead on to the road into Sidmouth behind a thatched house. Follow the road down on the right-hand side, until you come to the old road, which was closed to traffic in 1997, following a cliff fall. Pass through a kissing gate and walk down the old road, through a gate at the lower

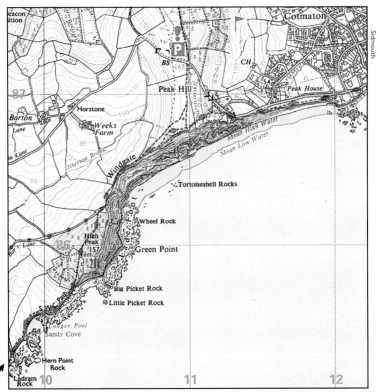

Contours are given in metres
The vertical interval is 5m

The sea front at Sidmouth, a popular resort since the early 19th century.

end and into the lawns which lead down to Jacob's Ladder. There is an award winning park on your right, with an intriguing restored WW2 pill box near the entrance. It does not lead through to the sea front, so to continue east you have to follow the pavement to the landward side of the sea edge houses. If you look up the road going inland here you will see Glen Lodge – the future Queen Victoria spent her childhood holidays here.

(For those coming from the east, follow the cliff top lawns as far as you can, then follow the route of the old road to the left (seaward) side of the new road. At the top go through a gate, and follow the road a short way up the hill, until you enter the woods up a short, steep staircase on your left, just past a thatched house.)

Sidmouth is a fine, restful, seaside resort which has succeeded in combining traditional charms with all the ingredients for a pleasant stay and little to disturb the passing walker. There are good views of the red cliffs of Peak Hill and Ladram to the west as you walk along the sea front. The fishermen sell some of their fresh catch just round the corner from their boats, which are tied up at the eastern end of the beach.

The scenery of nearby Heritage Coasts attracts visitors to resorts such as Budleigh Salterton.

Conserving the Dorset and East Devon Coasts

The Coast Path is formally designated by the Countryside Commission with the blessing of the government. The Path is managed by Devon and Dorset County Councils with substantial financial help from the Commission.

Much of the countryside through which the Path runs has been formally designated as an Area of Outstanding Natural Beauty by the Commission. This gives national recognition to the high quality of the landscape.

Heritage Coasts and the Future

The idea of special measures for protecting the rural coast became a matter of some urgency just before the Second World War, when the ever-quickening pace of development was already beginning to destroy the beauty of parts of Britain's rural coastline.

During the War the government appointed Professor Steers, the eminent coastal geographer, to assess the scenic quality of the undeveloped coastline of England and Wales.

It was more than twenty years before the government set in motion an official review. In 1970 the Countryside Commission reported back with a major proposal that 'the most scenically outstanding stretches of undeveloped coast be defined and protected as Heritage Coasts'.

Much of the coast of Dorset and Devon is defined as Heritage Coast by the Commission in association with local authorities, thus affording it special protection through planning with a strong emphasis on practical action. Heritage Coast teams work with parish councils, landowners, farmers, voluntary organisations and individuals to coordinate a wide range of conservation and recreation tasks and to help in the management of the South West Coast Path to ensure that the coastal environment is well looked after.

It is an exciting time for coastal management. The pioneering model of the Heritage Coasts is now being extended to the wider coastline. Management is being achieved by cooperation between coastal interests through voluntary groups such as the Dorset Coast Forum and the Lyme Bay Forum. Coastal managers are being encouraged to 'look out to the sea' and consider the *whole* coast as an ecologically integrated entity.

The National Trust and Enterprise Neptune
The National Trust (NT) was founded in 1895 as a non-profit-making voluntary association independent of government, and acquires land and buildings which are of national importance in order to protect them.

In 1965 the Trust launched its operation 'Enterprise Neptune', the aim of which was to acquire as much as possible of the most beautiful stretches of coastline in England and Wales. The Trust made further appeals and now owns one-third of the rural coast of Dorset.

The National Trust's efforts are complementary to those of the Heritage Coast teams. The latter work with all the owners and occupiers, while the National Trust operation gives the added protection that only ownership can ensure.

English Nature
This is the official organisation responsible for wildlife conservation and geologically important sites in England. It is also responsible for advising government.

Sites of special scientific interest (SSSIs) are designated by English Nature with strict guidelines being laid down for their protection. Virtually the whole of this coast is designated as SSSI, primarily for its geological interest, but in addition for the accompanying flora and fauna.

English Nature is also responsible for National Nature Reserves (NNRs). You will pass two major ones, at the undercliffs between Axmouth and Lyme Regis, and at Studland.

The Devon and Dorset wildlife trusts
These trusts manage numerous reserves along the path which are mentioned in the route description. Both these organisations also give much help and advice to those who are involved in the day to day management of this coastline.

The British Trust for Conservation Volunteers (BTCV)
This trust, and its affiliated local voluntary groups in each county, have carried out much of the practical conservation work on these coasts over the past 20 years.

The Royal Society for the Protection of Birds (RSPB)
The RSPB manages reserves at Radipole and Lodmoor in Weymouth and at Arne on the southern shores of Poole Harbour.

The red sandstone stacks of Ladram Bay.

By giving guidance on their subject they have played a major role in preventing threats to bird life.

European conservation award
From personal experience I can say that the co-operation of landowners, farmers, local authorities, the various amenity and civic societies of town and villages along the route, and many hundreds of individuals has been a prime factor in the success in protecting the coastline along which this path runs.

3 Sidmouth to Beer

through Branscombe
$8\frac{1}{4}$ *miles (13.25 km)*

Leaving Sidmouth, cross the River Sid on an ornate footbridge by the fishing boats at the eastern end of the beach. Go straight uphill as far as you can and then turn left and inland to the first street parallel with the cliffs. Turn right into that street, which bears sharp left at the end. Then turn right and right again and rejoin the original cliff path up to Salcombe Hill.

Salcombe Hill is a good viewpoint with easy access from a car park. (See the circular walk described on page 43.) At the edge of the plateau there is a direction finder and viewpoint **9**.

In the next valley is Salcombe Mouth, a secluded shingle beach accessible by a steep path. Beer Head comes into sight and the yellow stripe of greensand (it is green when first exposed) identifies Higher Dunscombe Cliff.

At Salcombe Mouth cross the stream by the footbridge just

Contours are given in metres
The vertical interval is 5m

back from the cliff and climb to Dunscombe Cliff. On reaching the top, cross several level fields up to a stile at the eastern end of the plateau where you come into sight of the Lincombe Valley. Pass to the landward side of this wild and overgrown hollow, keeping more or less on the level. About 400 yards (365 metres) inland drop down to a stile to rise briefly on the other side and regain your original height.

The path meanders through many old lime pits **10** before coming close to the edge of Lower Dunscombe Cliff. A zigzag path through Dunscombe Coppice and the meadow below then connects the cliff top and Weston Mouth.

Weston Combe is a valley of hedgerows, small fields and wild flowers. Weston Mouth has a shingle beach with a few weathered chalets nestling among the windswept undergrowth. The path descends to the beach briefly before rising back up a gully to the low cliff top which, on both sides of the valley, is owned by the National Trust. A climb to the east brings the path to the top of Weston Cliff.

The path stays near Weston Cliff for the length of one old field

Contours are given in metres
The vertical interval is 5m

at the western end and then strikes diagonally across the next field, the boundary of which is marked now only by a bank and a few bushes. It then passes to the landward side of a small hanging valley, Littlecombe Hollow, and through a gateway and then a stile, to emerge into a large, open field. Follow the cliff top slopes, cross a low, stony bank the western rampart of Berry Cliff Camp (see Pre Roman times on the coast p. 114), and after another 500 yards (450 metres) the easternmost bank to descend into an area of overgrown woodland which has colonised the old chalk pits behind Branscombe **11** (see page 44 for a circular walk in this area). Go left and then right to follow the well-defined track which keeps parallel with the cliffs.

Branscombe Church soon comes into view and is well worth a visit. A public footpath leads down to the church and nearby is the village post office where you can buy soft drinks and basic refreshments.

At Branscombe continue directly eastwards where the route enters National Trust property and a junction by a stile allows you to descend to the village mill **12** (NT) and the Masons Arms,

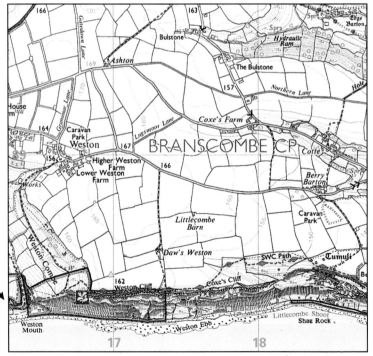

Contours are given in metres
The vertical interval is 5m

should you require refreshment. Meanwhile the Coast Path continues straight on, and you cross two stiles. Just before dropping into the scrub there is a fine clifftop view of Hooken Cliff and Under Hooken to the east.

Near Branscombe Mouth keep just inland of the coastguard cottages which have now become a hotel. At Branscombe Mouth there is a café and car park next to the shingle beach.

From here, to go towards Beer, you cross a small footbridge and one field. You then have a choice. You can either drop down into Under Hooken, and climb out of the eastern end, or

Contours are given in metres
The vertical interval is 5m

you can keep to the cliff top until the paths reunite. There is no official public right of way along the clifftop until just east of the old coastguard lookout, although there is a well used path. Now the route hugs the cliff and finally goes across to join a small lane which runs along the seaward edge of a caravan site, and down the road to the fishing village of Beer.

(If you are going west, go up Common Lane. At the top, go to the seaward side of the car park (Little Lane) and the caravan site. Just after the headland look for a stile which gives access to the undercliff at Hooken and the lower path to Branscombe Mouth.)

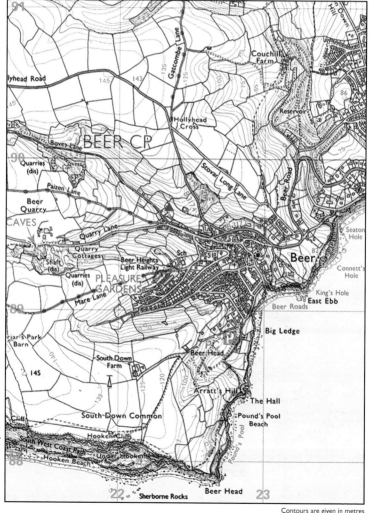

Contours are given in metres
The vertical interval is 5m

A CIRCULAR WALK AT SALCOMBE HILL

2½ miles (3.9 km) (see maps on pages 38–9)

To reach Salcombe Hill car park **13**, where the walk starts, leave the Lyme Regis to Exeter A3052 road at the signs for Salcombe Regis. Keep to the road markings and follow signs for Sidmouth, passing north of Thorn Farm, formerly the seat of the Manor Court, and the Salcombe Thorn, carefully preserved by the village since the welfare of the community is believed to depend on its health. Just over half a mile (1 km) past the Salcombe Thorn you will see the car park.

At the back of the car park you will see a waymarked route leading south. Follow this and take the first left turning from it. Go straight on at each of the junctions and soon you will come into sight of thatched buildings across the valley to the right. Keep going and you will soon see the church of St Peter and St Mary and the village of Salcombe Regis straight ahead up the wooded valley. On reaching the village continue up the lane to Salcombe Church which has many 15th century features.

For Salcombe Mouth come out of the church and retrace your steps down the hill, but keep to the surfaced lane until just before the road branches slightly left for Coombe Wood Farm.

Turn right here through a kissing gate and almost straight away leave the field track to go through a second kissing gate to continue down the side of the valley, keeping the hedge to your left. The narrow path goes straight ahead through a meadow and small field and then turns left into the valley bottom by a farm shed. Now follow the stream down to the sea at Salcombe Mouth. There are steep steps leading down to a secluded shingle beach. To continue, turn westward towards Sidmouth along the Coast Path. During the steep climb west you may see bluebells, speedwell and red campion in the spring.

At the top of a flight of steps there is a junction with a path leading inland. Carry straight on along the Coast Path through a wide bridle gate and past the South Coombe Farm memorial stone. From the National Trust donations cairn and a direction finder follow the wide, flat, grassy path back inland to the Salcombe Hill car park.

Route to Salcombe Hill cliff for elderly or infirm people: park in the same place as for the previous walk but, instead of following the directions above to Salcombe Regis, follow Southdown Drive and keep going seaward all the way to the cliff top, and return by retracing your steps.

A CIRCULAR WALK AT BRANSCOMBE
2½ miles (4.2 km) (see map on page 41)

Park at the village hall car park **14**, turn right and follow the road up towards the church. After about 100 yards you will come to the village post office and the 16th century 'Church Living' on your right with the church on your left. Much of the structure is Norman. There is a 15th century wagon roof and the screen, gallery and altar rails are all Jacobean. The 18th century pulpit has three tiers. There are several fine memorials, one of which commemorates the Wadham family who lived just up the road at Edge Barton and founded Wadham College, Oxford.

Coming out of the church door go straight ahead through the churchyard and across the valley into the woods. Steps lead up through the woods and, shortly after climbing a stile near the top, you come to a well-defined track. Turn right (west) and continue along this wooded track until you see an open meadow on the northern, landward side with a farm track leading across the middle.

Follow this farm track inland and bear left to keep the woodland ahead to your right. At the end of the second field the path enters the woods and descends diagonally to Street, with the Fountain Head pub and a group of cottages. Make your way past the pub and facing you at the end of the lane is a gateway with a track rising steeply through it towards the right. After passing several chalk outcrops and rising into a meadow at the top, bear left towards the woods ahead and enter them through a bridle gate.

Go diagonally left across the copper ore pits **15** and follow the track at the far side north and inland for about 110 yards. Here fork right off the track on to a path down through the woods which will bring you into a narrow lane. Keep going inland on the same side of the valley to Hole House.

Turn down in front of the house to the bottom of the valley. After crossing the stream keep on up the lane which bends slightly right, and then take the hairpin bend backwards to return down the valley. Continue past Woodhouse Farm to join the lane which will shortly take you back to the village hall.

Branscombe village was once the scene of a considerable cottage industry, based on the wool trade.

The wool trade

All the way along this path there are small villages apparently with no great source of wealth or industry. Yet beautifully decorated parish churches or substantially built stately homes of other centuries are evidence of past wealth.

From early medieval times, the hinterland of this coast was found to be an excellent place for agriculture in general and in particular for the breeding of sheep for wool. Most of the agricultural products of the hinterland would have been used for home consumption, but a number of developments in the wool trade led to a thriving export industry which was to bring great wealth to the coastal ports of Dorset and East Devon.

Edward III did much to encourage the spinning and weaving of cloth when he forbade the export of raw wool. As time went on, the immigration of Flemish weavers and the French Huguenots helped to develop cloth manufacture of a high quality.

In the beginning the industry would have been supplied with enough sheep locally to enable the manufacturers to have extremely low raw material costs. The great abbeys, which owned large tracts of land along the route covered by this path, notably Glastonbury, Bindon, Forde, Sherborne and Abbotsbury, would have derived much of their income from their agricultural estates. The evidence of their wealth can still

Cliffs near Sidmouth.

be seen, particularly at Abbotsbury through which the Coast Path passes.

Initially the spinning and weaving was an urban industry, with the countryside merely supplying the wool. However, at some time around 1400 the industry began to take over rural sites, where there was water power, previously used only for grinding corn.

Many of these medieval mills have left traces or are even standing today. A recent study showed that in Dorset every mill which can still be traced was already in action at the time of Domesday in 1086.

The old method of treating wool cloth was to tread on the cloth in a tank of water, and this demanded relatively little water. The treatment of cloth by the new method of 'fulling' (treating the cloth mechanically) needed mechanical power, so many mills were converted to the new, more lucrative, work. Traditionally, the villagers would have made cloth in their cottages and probably sold any surpluses in the towns. Thus it was not difficult for the new mill owners to find skilled labour out in the country.

Cottage industry would have been a feature of nearly all the villages through which the Coast Path passes, but often there is little evidence of it in the architecture. However, at Branscombe you may notice three-storey cottages near the old mill. They are often an indication of the weaving industry, with looms being located on the top floor for extra light.

The industry would have had its ups and downs from the medieval period until the early 19th century, and one mill might have changed its trade from cloth to corn several times according to the prevailing economics. With the huge increase in trade in the 19th century, however, the small streams and rivers that served the mills near this coast were no longer able to supply enough power to meet the growing demand. Gradually the cloth industry moved away to the north, where steam power from coal was almost limitless.

Hand-made Dorset buttons

This great cottage industry of the 18th and early 19th centuries employed many women and children, and two coastal villages which obtained a reputation for their buttons were Wool and Langton Matravers. The collapse of the Dorset button trade from the mid 19th century was caused by the rise of button-making in the industrial midlands.

The River Axe near Seaton.

4 Beer to Lyme Regis

over Axe Bridge and past Culverhole Point
8¾ miles (14 km)

Above the beach and opposite the Anchor Inn in Beer follow the
surfaced path which starts on a more or less level course and
keeps to the cliff top, overlooking the fishing boats pulled up on
the pebbles. Keep to the cliff top for 400 yards. The path leads
into a narrow lane. Turn sharp right down this to a post box and
telephone kiosk by Seaton Hole. At low tide you can go down
the steep path and walk along the beach to the sea front path at
the Chine. Otherwise follow the cliff top road east, keep straight
ahead for about 600 yards (540 metres) to the far end of a large
terrace of houses on the right. Near the end of these is a footpath
sign pointing towards the sea. Follow this, turn left at the sea
front and continue to the bridge at Axmouth.

(If walking from the east you should follow the sea front as far
as you can. Then turn up the path to the Beer road. Turn left to
Seaton Hole. Take the lane for 70 yards (65 metres) and look for
the path on the left, going backwards slightly to start with.)

Axmouth, two-thirds of a mile (1 km) upstream from the

Contours are given in feet
The vertical interval is 25ft

The wharf at Axmouth, which is an attractive village well worth a detour.

bridge and harbour, is a pleasant old village with some thatched cottages, inns and accommodation; the church is worth a detour. There is tent camping at Axe Farm, in the field right opposite.

Note that the old bridge over the Axe **16**, still standing beside the new one, is one of the earliest concrete bridges still surviving, built in 1877, but disguised as a masonry bridge.

Just north of the bridge is a sign 'Welcome to Axe Bridge Golf Club'. The Coast Path follows the lane past the old coastguard cottages and passes to the landward side of the club house. Through the golf course keep straight up a valley until you come to a narrow track, with views back towards Beer Head, the westernmost chalk cliffs of the south coast.

Two hundred yards up this lane, opposite a stile for the path to Axmouth village, the Coast Path turns off right (south), as a narrow grassy track between hedges. In the next fields go diagonally left (south-east) before following the edge of the fields just outside and above the reserve until the entrance point which is clearly indicated with an information sign. I am now going to describe the path as it was in August 1995; you may find that it has changed in part since then because of further landslips. The wardens keep a route waymarked through the area, so always follow their signs rather than adhering slavishly to this guide (see page 58 for further information about the reserve).

Remember that once you enter the reserve it is 6 miles (10 km) to the other end. Some of this walking can be demanding, particularly if it has rained recently and the paths are slippery on the steeper slopes. The only way out is to retrace your steps or to continue to Lyme Regis. There are no public access points along the way.

The path passes through almost jungle-like woodland for the whole way, but from time to time magnificent views will open up through gaps in the trees. If you walk quietly you may see some roe deer and other animals.

Not far to the east of the reserve entrance the path follows the ridge of a natural bank with a chasm to the landward side which probably formed about 200 years ago.

This bank is the result of a classic rotational slip where the weight of the descending rock and soil on the landward side has actually pushed this great mound of material upwards.

A little further east again the path emerges to give one last glimpse of Beer Head before diving back into the undergrowth.

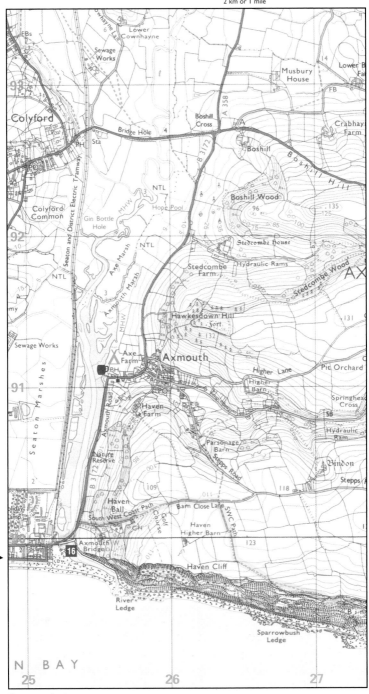

Contours are given in metres
The vertical interval is 5m

When a clear view of the sea next opens out you will see the cliff face of 'Goat Island' **17**. The area below this is called Culverhole Gully, and there were once plans to establish a harbour here. Just to the east is Culverhole Point. The path again dives into the undergrowth and below the ash trees with their abundance of ivy and the rope-like lianas of traveller's joy. Hart's tongue fern is abundant and in spring red campion provides spots of colour in the dense, dark green undergrowth. The sun only filters through in the clearings and the sky is seen in glimpses through the quivering ash leaves above.

Soon you will find that the path east of this winds up and down for a short way before coming on to another ridge, through what could almost be an avenue of sycamore trees, with similar ridges on either side as far as you can see through the dense undergrowth. The way then enters a small opening and begins to go up and down again. Privet and wood spurge, stinking iris, dog's mercury and the hart's tongue fern are among the multitude of plants that cover the ground.

About ten minutes' walk to the east you may notice a recently made clearing, created by the reserve wardens to diversify the habitat. This was once the garden of Critchard's Cottage, abandoned in the 1839 landslip. The hazel you see growing around here is what remains of hazel coppicing, carried on at the undercliff until the 1950s.

Just to the east you may notice the ruins of Cliff Cottage, which replaced Critchard's Cottage and was lived in until 1950 by the Gappers. Annie Gapper used to serve cream teas to visitors in this delightful setting **18**.

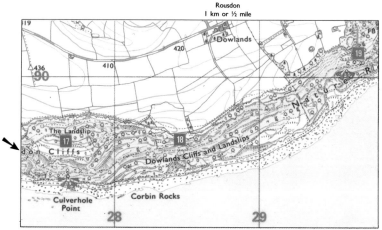

Rousdon
1 km or ½ mile

Contours are given in feet
The vertical interval is 25ft

Half an hour's walk east from here you will find another national nature reserve information sign **19** and map, where a private track comes down from the landward side. This is roughly the halfway point. The ruins here are the remains of an old pumping station.

The path follows the track over the bridge and soon branches off seaward to mount a long flight of wooden steps upwards through a tunnel of hawthorn and hazel coppice, to emerge on a small peak **20** overlooking Charton Bay, not so long ago a favourite landing place for smugglers, with Humble Point just to the east.

The route east of Whitlands Cliff is narrow and clings to the side of a steep slope overlooking a chasm full of bracken.

Once again the path emerges on to a ridge with a small chasm below and 100-foot (30-metre) high cliffs topped by a yellow outcrop of greensand above.

When you see a concrete block inscribed 'CR' (Combpyne Rousden is the name of the parish) you are approaching Whitlands Cliff. The path is now well back from the sea and occasionally you will catch glimpses over the enormous 1840 landslip, with Humble Green culminating in Humble Rocks and Humble Point below.

The path now meanders up and down the relatively old and stable-looking landslips. Soon you will come to the ruins of an old cottage, of which the garden can still be traced, and parts of which still stand two storeys high. West Cliff Cottage was built in about 1830 and collapsed only years later in 1840.

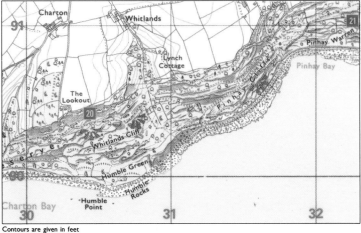

Contours are given in feet
The vertical interval is 25ft

Just east of this you will see holm oak and beech trees as well as turkey oak and sycamore. Soon the path drops down to a small pumping station.

The right of way shown going south here subsided and became impassable, so follow the tarmac track from the water pumping station which climbs steadily east for well over a quarter of a mile. After the same distance again the tarmac ends and the Coast Path forks seawards. After the junction the path crosses a small rivulet and a massive recent landslip, which is a good illustration of the process of rotational slip, with its very recently pushed-up ridges and deep cracks in the soil.

From Ware Cliffs the view opens up and you will see an area of great turmoil where the trees lie twisted and broken like matchsticks all the way down to the sea **21**. To the east of this landslip can sometimes be seen ponds which often form between the banks of rotational slips. These make the area even more unstable, as the water held in them seeps into the soil and helps to cause the next slip.

Contours are given in feet
The vertical interval is 25ft

The wall of The Cobb, the harbour of Lyme Regis.

About ten minutes' walk to the east of all this there is a stile, and after another 100 yards you reach the nature reserve boundary sign and a small lane parallel to the coast, and go past a bungalow on the landward side of the path with a wicket gate opposite, through which the Coast Path leads. Across the fields a very substantial hedge with yet another wicket gate passing through it forms the boundary between Devon and Dorset.

To the east of the county boundary the path crosses open meadows (NT) and a small stream. At the back of the woods immediately above The Cobb there is a stile with steps that emerge at the bowling green beside The Cobb, the harbour of Lyme.

The Cobb, of medieval origin, has witnessed many dramas of English history. The most famous of the recorded epics began with the support given by Lyme to the defeat of the Armada as it appeared off this coast one day in 1588. In the same century the man who discovered the Bahamas, Sir George Somers, was born in Lyme and in 1644 The Cobb again played a vital role when the Royalist troops besieged the town from the land.

Lyme continued to be supplied from the sea and successfully saw off the Royalists. The Restoration of the monarchy in 1660 was therefore not welcome in this town. Religious services had to be held illegally in the surrounding countryside, including on the cliffs above what is now the national nature reserve, and when the Duke of Monmouth arrived (near Monmouth Beach **22**) 25 years later he was welcomed and proclaimed king here, and gathered many supporters armed with their pitchforks. The savage repression of this rebellion was one of the factors in the success of the Protestant William of Orange, when three years later he landed in Britain further west along the South West Coast Path at Torbay, and became king.

The Axmouth–Lyme Regis Undercliffs National Nature Reserve

The reserve was set up by the Nature Conservancy Council in 1955/6 and contains one of the largest and best examples of land-slipping in the British Isles.

In very simplified terms there are three layers of rocks and soils here. Chalk layers 100 feet high sit on top of greensand, and these two let water through, with a waterproof base of clays which slopes slightly towards the sea.

When it rains two events occur. The upper layers get waterlogged, their many thousands of tons of dry weight become millions of tons, and the wet clay becomes quite slippery. Thus the material above starts sliding, in this case seawards, producing the landscape you now see.

A particularly well-reported case of this slipping, which is an almost constant process, occurred at Christmas 1839. The people who lived and worked there at the time thought it was an earthquake, so dramatic was the sudden movement, and contemporary accounts and melodramatic drawings are on display in the Lyme Regis museum.

One notable feature of this slip, which is at the far Axe Bridge end of the reserve, is that a large block of land was completely isolated from its neighbouring fields and yet retained its level top, complete with a crop of wheat and turnips, divided from firm land by a dramatic chasm. This became something of a tourist attraction at the time and Queen Victoria came to observe the scene from her Royal Yacht. The chasm is three-quarters of a mile (1.2 km) long, and 200 feet (60 metres) deep. The area still remains, called 'Goat Island' **17**, and is now part of the reserve.

Lyme Regis and the surrounding countryside

Those who have read Jane Austen will recognise features of the harbour and the small town huddled on the cliffs opposite which she describes in *Persuasion*.

There is a marine aquarium on The Cobb, where local fishermen bring unusual finds, and I recommend a visit to the museum and the 15th century Parish Church of St Michael the

Dense undergrowth is a feature of the Undercliffs National Nature Reserve.

Archangel, which has a number of 12th and 13th century features, a mixture which gives the interior a most intriguing and unusual appearance.

The Cobb was probably first built as a wooden structure in the 13th century, and for several centuries Lyme Regis was an important and prosperous outlet for the wool trade of the rich towns of Somerset. In the 17th century there was even trade with the American colonies and the West Indies.

In the middle of the 18th century, however, the economy of this area was at a low ebb and one ship a month was leaving for America with emigrants. Things picked up later and the harbour records show that 600 ships a year used the port during the early 19th century, and that nearly 40 of the ships operated from Lyme. During the Napoleonic wars, regular fortnightly sailings to the Channel Islands were instituted. In 1830 Lyme had been made a bonding port, and just behind The Cobb the Custom House sits alongside other contemporary warehouses. Shipbuilding also thrived here well into the 19th century.

The tourist industry also came to the rescue and, with the help of Jane Austen and other more recent writers, the holiday trade has been thriving ever since. Although The Cobb attracts little commercial trade these days, it still helps to protect Lyme from erosion and provides a safe haven for fishing and sailing boats.

5 Lyme Regis to Bridport

through Charmouth and Seatown
9½ miles (15.25 km)

Following negotiations with Lyme golf Club over access to cliffs, the Dorset County Council has bought land to enable the path once again to follow the cliff top to Charmouth. To rejoin the path care must be taken not to venture onto any of the rights of way marked on the map across The Spittles, a landslip area which is currently almost continuously dangerous. Landslides occur without notice and the mud flows can be lethal.

From the bridge by the Museum pass the traffic lights and make for the church. Keep walking up the street and past the Charmouth Road car park **23**. Opposite the cemetery above that, there is a small lane with a stile set in the hedge between the entrance of this lane and the main road to Charmouth.

From the stile, the Coast Path goes diagonally across the fields into a small lane where you have to turn west for a few yards (this is not a mistake and nobody has turned the sign round). Then turn northeast once again to go through the beech planta-

The busy town of Lyme Regis, a fashionable resort in the 18th century and still a tourist attraction.

tion and up the steps towards Timber Hill (NT). This brings you to the top of the cliff which is followed for about threequarters of a mile (1 km).

Towards Charmouth this cliff-top path goes into a small lane. Take the first junction seawards off this lane and this soon comes to the cliff top again to descend to Charmouth Beach. This last section can be susceptible to cliff falls; if the path is closed please follow the waymarked diversions. Once at the beach, you will find the Charmouth Heritage Coast Centre **24** and car park. This centre has a warden/geologist who gives guided walks. The main theme of the centre is the geology of the area and I can heartily recommend a visit.

The barn-like building by the beach at Charmouth is an old cement works. You can still see the lime kiln remains behind it.

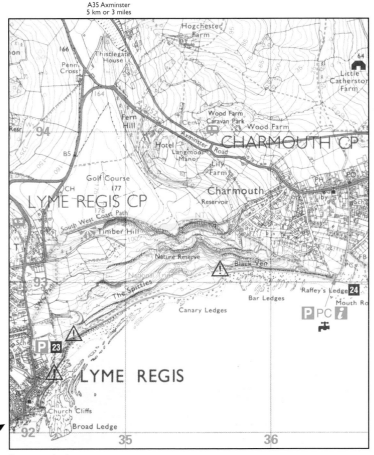

Contours are given in metres
The vertical interval is 5m

From the Charmouth Heritage Coast Centre **24** the official route goes up the road and then follows a lane to the right to cross a wooden footbridge. Then it keeps to the cliff top all the way to Golden Cap. Most of the land is owned by the National Trust which keeps the route open when another chunk of the cliffs slips into the sea. From Charmouth there is an energetic climb to the top of the cliff which is called Cain's Folly on the maps.

At Cain's Folly the path stays fairly level for the length of three fields and comes to a junction which connects the Coast Path with the National Trust car park on Stonebarrow Hill. Look out for the signs outside the National Trust shop which show waymarked walks around the Golden Cap Estate.

The main route, however, keeps straight ahead and drops down steeply to the lower cliffs below Westhay Farm, continuing to cling to the seaward edge of the fields.

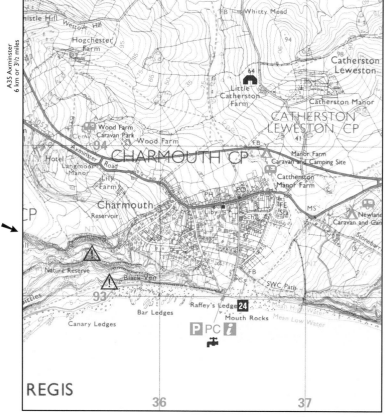

Contours are given in metres
The vertical interval is 5m

Lyme Regis and Charmouth from Cain's Folly.

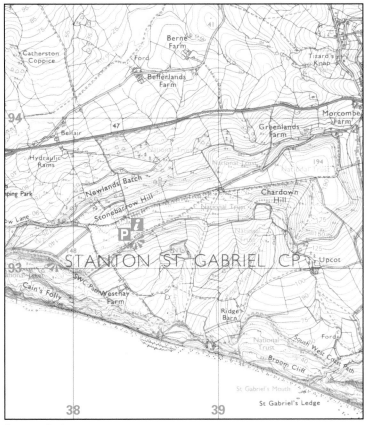

Contours are given in metres
The vertical interval is 5m

Just west of Golden Cap, the highest point on the south coast of England, at 626 feet (190 metres), the path drops into a small hollow, crosses a bridge and then rises across a field to rejoin the cliff top, which it follows until it crosses a stile giving entrance to the heather-covered peak of Golden Cap.

You may like to make a small diversion here, leaving the Coast Path just before the bridge mentioned above, into what was the village of St Gabriel's **25**. Go to the landward side of the cottages in St Gabriel's and up a small trackway towards Golden Cap. There you will see the remains of St Gabriel's Church. In former times the main road, now destroyed by erosion, came through the village of St Gabriel's, which was a thriving community.

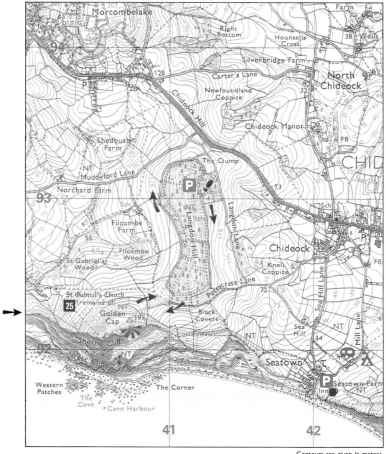

Contours are given in metres
The vertical interval is 5m

From the church ruins make straight for the steep slopes of Golden Cap. The path zigzags up to a small, flat, grassy plateau with a memorial to the past Chairman of the National Trust, the Earl of Antrim, and continues east to the trig point. Here it goes northwards and inland down the steep slope before branching eastwards once again along a hedgerow. Follow the hedgerow parallel to the cliff top, cross a field immediately south of Langdon Hill, then keep straight on to the beach at Seatown.

In the summer, it may be possible to cross the small river at Seatown by staying on the beach. Otherwise, follow the official route which is inland a short distance and crosses a bridge.

From Seatown climb up to Ridge Cliff and pass just behind Doghouse Hill. Then you have the choice of passing behind Thorncombe Beacon or keeping to the cliff top, which is more strenuous but offers magnificent views.

The descent between Thorncombe Beacon and Eype Mouth is straightforward. At Eype Mouth there is a small car park. The village is a quarter of a mile (400 metres) inland with a hotel and inn. The post office is no longer open.

Cross Eype Mouth by the stepping stones, and stay by the cliff all the way to the top of the hill called West Cliff. The path

Contours are given in metres
The vertical interval is 5m

passes to the landward side of some limestone workings and the ruins of a lime kiln **26**, and crosses a field diagonally to the cliff top. The path then follows the cliff to West Bay. If you wish to visit Bridport **27**, you can simply follow the signs up the Brit River Valley and along paths which pass a thatched brewery **28** on the way.

A circular walk at Golden Cap
1.9 miles (3 km) (see map on page 64)

The car park on this walk is difficult to find. On the main A35 Bridport to Lyme Regis road there is a short piece of dual carriageway at the top of the steep hill west of Chideock.

At the Chideock end of this dual carriageway a small lane strikes seaward next to a lay-by. Take this lane and a sign will be seen almost immediately pointing left to the Langdon Hill car park. Park by the information displays and NT donations cairn.

The tracks which go in either direction encircle the forestry of Langdon Hill, so proceed to the seaward end of Langdon Hill immediately behind Golden Cap.

Here you will see a small path leading through a squeezer stile directly towards Golden Cap. Cross the fields and after a short steep climb to the top of the Cap enjoy the outstanding views.

Retrace your steps back to the track and follow it in the opposite direction to the one from which you came, back to the car park.

This is an easy walk and, with the exception of the last section up Golden Cap, is level, so it can be tackled by people of any age. Glimpses of the old, well-conserved hedgerows of the National Trust property to the west make a fine foreground to the views of Lyme Regis and Devon in the background.

To the east can be seen Thorncombe Beacon which bears some resemblance to Golden Cap because of its similar geological structure. Beyond that the pier of Bridport Harbour (renamed West Bay by the railway company when it arrived in the 19th century) is quite close. Further off can be seen the wide sweep of the Chesil Bank and the limestone mass of Portland.

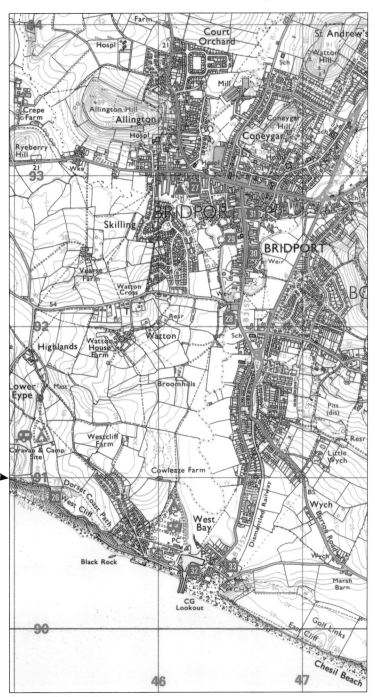

Contours are given in metres
The vertical interval is 5m

67

Bridport town

Bridport is a small rural market town which has retained many of its traditional shop fronts and has not yet been affected by the 'redevelopment' schemes which have destroyed many of the towns of England to the east. It is therefore an ideal place to spend a day or two.

It is the home of the rope-making industry and for centuries has supplied fishing nets to many countries of the world as well as the ropes for shipping.

There are many pubs and tea houses along the main street of the town, and the holiday trade has been an important part of Bridport's economy for 100 years.

In South Street there is the particularly fine medieval parish church of St Mary **29**. A little way south of this are the almshouses and courtyard of the Friends' Meeting House **30**. The almshouses are 15th and 16th century town houses with a spiral stone staircase leading out of a courtyard. The story is that the main meeting room was a barn, and that the owner permitted the then illegal Quaker worshippers to meet there in secret.

The courtyard of the Friends' Meeting House, Bridport.

In any event the owner, Daniel Taylor, gave the Meeting House to the Society of Friends in 1697 and the adjoining buildings were handed over to trustees as almshouses. A visit is recommended.

A hundred yards further south is the 15th century chantry, possibly an ancient defensive building, and beyond that the thatched brewery with its waterwheel by the River Brit.

In a medieval building near the town centre there is the Bridport Museum **31**, with good displays illustrating many facets of Bridport's fascinating history.

Bridport's industries

Ropes for the navy and fishing nets

This is the one industry with medieval origins that is still thriving on the Dorset coast. The fields around Bridport were ideal for growing flax for ropes as early as the 13th century.

Much of the local wealth indicated by the good-quality housing of past centuries, as well as by beautiful churches in Bridport and the villages surrounding it, derives either from the wool trade or from the rope and net industries.

Some of the coastal villages which were involved both with growing hemp and with assistance in the manufacturing process were Eype, Chideock, Burton Bradstock and Abbotsbury. Hemp growing died out during the 19th century when it became cheaper to buy supplies from Italy and Russia.

About 200 years ago Bridport also started to make sail cloth, and the neighbouring inland town of Beaminster joined in. The flax needed for it continued to be grown by Dorset farmers, and inland at Beaminster the manufacture of sail cloth replaced the local wool trade before the end of the 19th century.

If you look carefully at the small alleyways beside many of the houses in Bridport you will see they have long narrow yards behind them. These are the 'ropewalks', where the ropes used to be made. Imagine the spinning and twisting being carried out in the long gardens, and the various products being hung out in the street to dry.

As rope-making began to take place on a larger scale elsewhere, the town adapted and began to concentrate on the production of nets of all varieties. Nowadays everything from trawler nets to football nets, billiard table pockets and tennis nets are made and exported to all parts of the world. Many of these products are still finished by hand, and so cottage industry is still alive in Bridport and its surrounding villages.

Man-made fibres, especially nylon, have taken over from natural materials but the industry continues to thrive in our own century.

Bridport Harbour 32

In Saxon and medieval times Bridport's harbour would probably have been quite close to the town centre. As you walk along the Chesil Beach you will notice that the river mouths there tend to get blocked by shingle thrown up by the sea. This must have been a problem in medieval times as well as today. Where there are gaps, these have usually been made by the Environment Agency to allow the water to escape.

In 1721 an Act of Parliament was passed to allow the diversion of the River Brit and the creation of a harbour immediately behind the Chesil Bank. This harbour was completed in 1744 and shipbuilding yards thrived there for nearly 150 years. They had a good reputation for their boats – fishing boats, customs cutters and even naval orders during the Napoleonic wars. This trade fell into decline in the latter part of the 19th century when iron ships began to replace wooden ones, and the last ship was launched from Bridport in 1879.

The West Dorset District Council is the harbour authority in this area and continues to maintain the port against all the odds. To clear the harbour, the River Brit is dammed with sluices until the valley behind is full of water. The sluices are then opened fully to allow a great surge of water to scour the pebbles from the harbour entrance, a system which has been working now for nearly 250 years.

The Bridport Railway

In 1857 a group of local merchants succeeded in linking Bridport Harbour with the main Dorchester to London railway line. With an eye on the tourist trade, the terminus was called West Bay, and the recently restored railway station 33 still stands just behind the beach with its cast-iron angle-bracket roof supports embellished with the letters 'BR'. The Company did not have very large funds for this venture and so some of the railway buildings along the route were existing structures rented from local landlords. A row of cottages known as 'Railway Cottages' in one of the villages along the way is clearly many centuries old and the roofs still retain their thatch. The Great Western Railway took over the running of the trains from the outset and the last service ran from Maiden Newton to Bridport in the 1970s.

Bridport Harbour at West Bay, renowned for its shipbuilding until the late 19th century.

6 Bridport to West Bexington

past Burton Bradstock and along Chesil Beach
5¼ miles (8.75 km)

From West Bay, make for the high cliffs at the eastern end of the beach and follow the steep path to the cliff top.

On coming within sight of the caravan site go down to the beach and follow the main track through the site to the main facilities. Go straight on inland to the end of a stone wall, and turn right (east) through the tent site. Where the camp site track bends sharp left there is a low stile on your right, which can be hidden by tents in summer. Go over this to cross the River Bride, turning down the other side to rejoin the cliff top path and continue east. Moves are now afoot (1998) to bring the Coast Path closer to the sea, avoiding the camp site, so look out for waymarks here.

You can also take a short-cut by following the river upstream

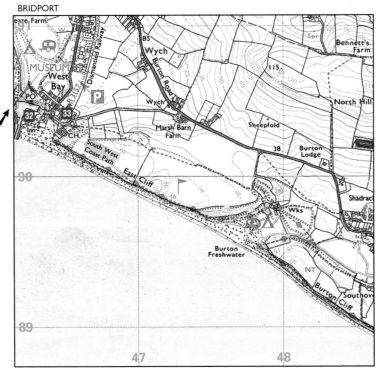

Contours are given in metres
The vertical interval is 5m

(left), having crossed the footbridge, until you come into a walled lane at the end of the village of Burton Bradstock. You then turn seaward over a stile and up the hill beside a stone wall to come back to the top of Burton Cliff.

Burton Bradstock, with an attractive 1825 Wesleyan chapel, is an interesting village which played a major part in the cloth industry, and a spinning mill operated from 1794 until 1931. In addition, the first flax 'swingling' mill in the West Country was built here and opened in 1803. To swingle flax means to dress it, by a beating process which breaks down the non-fibrous parts of the stems of the flax. After this the flax stems are drawn through a kind of comb (a 'hackle') to give the long strands of fibre that make linen. The church **34** is also attractive, built mainly during the 14th and 15th centuries.

The cliff top on the western side of Burton Beach overhangs in places, and for safety the Coast Path has been taken back a little way from the cliff. Keep back from the cliff just before descending the rocky path which arrives at Burton Beach (NT).

On the eastern side of Burton Beach the path follows a stone wall and again keeps back from the cliff. Trampling feet on the immediate cliff top were causing serious erosion.

The Path then leads into the Old Coastguard caravan site. Make your way across this, keeping close to the cliff until it drops down on to Cogden Beach.

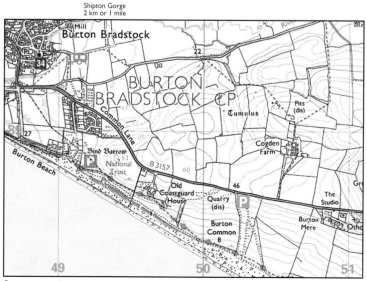

Contours are given in metres
The vertical interval is 5m

Cogden Beach is part of the famous Chesil Beach or Chesil Bank. The official route of the Coast Path passes to the landward side of the small lake here, but this is often flooded and difficult and most walkers will go to the seaward side of it. The route to West Bexington is actually on the pebbles of the Chesil Beach. It is extremely wearing and you often seem to take two paces forward and one back when walking this section, so allow extra time.

As you near West Bexington the fields may be flooded inland, and just before reaching the car park there is a large reed bed which is a nature reserve of the Dorset Wildlife Trust.

The great coastal monasteries

The path passes close to the ruins of parts of two very powerful medieval monasteries, at Abbotsbury, and further on at Little Bindon on the eastern side of Lulworth Cove (see page 76).

Abbotsbury

It is known that late Roman Britain was Christian, and it is possible that some of the Britons continued Christian traditions after the Roman withdrawal. It may be, therefore, that a church of St Peter was established during that time.

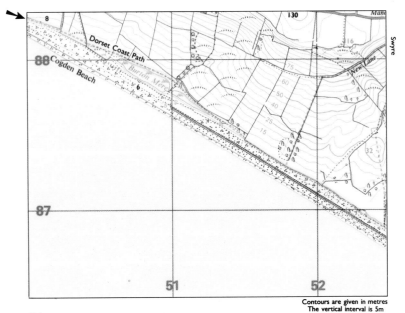

Contours are given in metres
The vertical interval is 5m

The Benedictine monastery was probably founded by monks from Cerne Abbas, just inland from Dorchester. We know there was a monastery here when William the Conqueror arrived, because Domesday gives us a detailed record of its wealth: there were eight manors, which included two mills, fifteen hectares of meadow, much woodland and 'land to sixteen ploughs'.

In the following centuries the aristocracy and kings of England offered their protection and made substantial donations of land and money. The Benedictine monasteries were academic centres and manuscripts show that the monks of Abbotsbury reached great heights in art and learning.

Charters were granted giving many rights and privileges, and inside the parish church, which was separate from the abbey church, you will find a drawing showing how the abbey would have looked at its greatest.

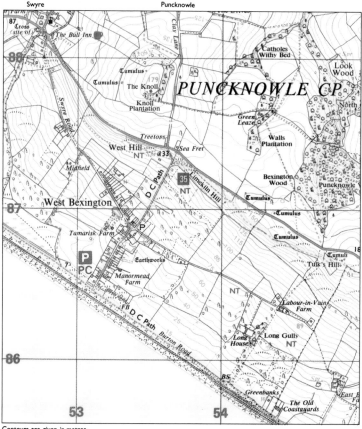

Contours are given in metres
The vertical interval is 5m

At this time there would have been people working wooden ploughs pulled by oxen on the hillsides above the village, where you can still see the terraced medieval fields.

During the 14th century there would also have been considerable building activity, with the sight of scaffolding around new stone buildings under construction. To the north of the abbey the village occupied approximately the same site as it does now, with its narrow streets leading to the market place where you will now find the village post office and the Ilchester Arms. A network of lanes would have radiated from the village to enable the abbot and his staff to go and supervise their farms, workshops and mills, and the lanes which lead off the main village street are the remnants of these ancient trackways.

In the 15th century the abbey appears to have gone through a period of great prosperity. It was then that the great Tithe Barn **53**, one of the largest in the country, was constructed, and this indicates that the agricultural production of the abbey and its associated establishments must have been considerable. St Catherine's Chapel **51**, on the hill above the village, was also built during this century and is worth a visit. It would appear, however, that in the late 1430s the abbot was letting the wealth of his domain lead to corrupt and dissolute habits. There were even hints that the abbot was not observing his vows of chastity.

At the beginning of the 16th century a gentleman called Thomas Strangways gave money for the establishment of a chantry so that the monks could pray for his soul daily, in perpetuity. Ironically, Henry VIII made Strangways' son Giles a commissioner for the Dissolution of the Dorset monasteries.

At the Dissolution the abbot became the vicar of the parish and Sir Giles Strangways was given a 20-year lease on the abbey with the condition that the buildings should be demolished.

This he did, converting part into a large house for himself and retaining the half of the Tithe Barn which still stands as a farm building. Much of the rest of the stonework of the abbey found its way into the houses in the village, as you will see when you walk along the village street.

The Abbey of Bindon

Cistercian monks arranged in 1149 to found a monastery at Lulworth Cove. The buildings on the eastern side of the Cove, at Little Bindon, which are immediately adjacent to the army range boundary, have been considered all that remains of the original foundation.

However, there is now some doubt about this. It is quite certain that an abbey was founded at Wool in 1172 and called Bindon. A charter of King John in 1216 set this out, and the buildings at Little Bindon, clearly medieval in origin, may have been established in association with the activities of the great abbey just inland. An aristocratic family called the de New-burghs, whose ancestors were personal friends of William the Conqueror, managed by the early 13th century to accumulate an estate which extended from Lulworth to Wool. In 1216 Robert de Newburgh granted land in three parishes to the abbey, and 17 years later made an additional grant of the eastern and southern part of the parish of West Lulworth, including the land around Lulworth Cove.

As the 13th century went on his son Henry made further substantial donations of land, and towards the end of the century many other landowners did likewise. The abbey came to possess farms in many villages of Dorset and controlled several thousand acres of land as well as some of the industrial sites of the time. Wareham fisheries are mentioned, and there is still a mill which was theirs on the River Frome, beside the London to Weymouth railway.

They owned water meadows (some of which still exist in the Frome Valley), put much of the more fertile land under the plough and used the downland for sheep pasture.

In the late 13th and 14th centuries, however, numerous disputes arose over ownership, payment of dues and land boundaries, and on occasion the disputes became bitter.

In the 15th century things seemed to have settled down considerably as far as the conflict between the abbey and the landowners was concerned, and an orderly system of small-holding for tenantry appears to have developed with a consequent rise in the fortunes of the abbey. The inventories prepared for the Dissolution by order of Henry VIII in 1539 showed that the abbots of Bindon were by then gaining a considerable income from leasing land for the grazing of sheep and other farming activities.

Two factors seem to have led to the demise of such abbeys. There was a threat from their power, which was often greater than that of the local landowners and aristocracy, and they were wealthy at a time when the king was short of cash. It would also seem that the religious intentions and piety of the monks and abbots was in doubt, and Henry VIII's argument with the Pope over his divorce was merely the last straw.

The 15th century Tithe Barn at Abbotsbury, with St Catherine's Chapel situated

...on the hill top.

7 West Bexington to Osmington Mills via the Ridgeway

past Abbotsbury Castle and Upwey
17 miles (27.25 km)

When the South West Coast Path was being established it was decided to have two alternative routes for the section from West Bexington to Osmington Mills, because one route had to satisfy the expectations that a coast path will stick to the coast. The strictly coastal route is therefore covered on pages 95–104.

In addition, it was thought a good idea to make the South Dorset Ridgeway available as an alternative. On clear days it has superb views of the sea and the Isle of Portland, as well as distant views of the hills of inland Dorset. It has also one of the most remarkable conglomerations of archaeological monuments in the whole of Britain. Even those who are not particularly interested in such things are likely to be impressed by views of Maiden Castle, one of the largest and most distinctive hill forts in Britain, as well as by the many other intriguing remains to be found along the route.

To follow the South Dorset Ridgeway (inland route) of the Coast Path go up the road above the beach car park at West Bexington. Where the road turns left, keep straight on up a narrow track, forking right just before the top. You will see a gateway on your right leading out on to the level meadow land of Limekiln Hill. This is National Trust land and they have restored the lime kiln with the help of the British Trust for Conservation Volunteers. You will find it just over the edge of the slope on the seaward side of the path **35**.

These lime kilns were once extensively used to produce lime for whitewash, plaster and mortar, or for reducing the acidity of some soils to improve cropping. Fuel and limestone would be unloaded from horse carts at the top end and the finished product would be extracted from the bottom. The coal used in this area was 'culm', a low-grade anthracite from Pembrokeshire. It was brought in by schooner, until rail transport arrived in the 19th century. During this century the production of lime has been concentrated on large centres, and cement produced in a few works has replaced the use of lime in building.

Now keep to the seaward edge of the meadow, cross the stone stile and keep straight on along the ridge towards a group of tumuli on the hill top. The path then follows the landward

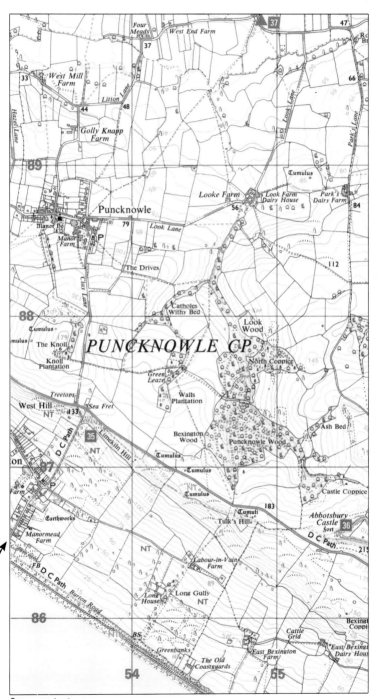

Four Meads
West End Farm
37
37
47
West Mill Farm
33
Litton Lane
44
48
Golly Knapp Farm
89
Tumulus
85
80
Looke Farm
Look Farm Dairy House
Park's Dairy Farm
84
Puncknowle
56
66
Manor Hs
79
Look Lane
P
Manor Farm
The Drives
112
Clay Lane
88
Catholes Withy Bed
Look Wood
Tumulus
mulus
The Knoll
North Coppice
145
Knoll Plantation
PUNCKNOWLE CP
Green Leaze
Treetops
Walls Plantation
West Hill
NT
433
Sea Fret
Ash Bed
DC Path
35
Bexington Wood
Puncknowle Wood
Limekiln Hill
NT
Tumulus
on
87
Castle Coppice
Farm
P
Cumulus
Cumulus
NT
Earthworks
Tumuli
183
Abbotsbury Castle
Manormead Farm
Tulk's Hill
Fort
36
DC Path
215
NT
Labour-in-Vain Farm
89
FB
DC Path
Burton Road
Long House
Long Gully
NT
Bexingt Coppi
86
Cattle Grid
BS
Bexington Dairy Hous
Greenbanks
The Old Coastguards
East Bexington Farm
54
55

Contours are given in metres
The vertical interval is 5m

81

side of a substantial dry stone wall until it crosses the Abbotsbury to Bridport road by a stile on the southern side of the road and a bridle gate on the northern side.

You now follow the southern ramparts of the Iron Age hill fort called Abbotsbury Castle **36**, and go straight across a small lane.

You can read more about these hill forts on page 114. This particular fort was never finished and its builders seem to have been in an enormous hurry. If you look carefully you will see that loads of soil were evidently dumped on the banks, but never levelled or finished in the normal way. Did the enemy arrive too soon? Was all this happening the day the Britons were losing against the Romans at Maiden Castle?

The lane mentioned above is an 'Unclassified County Road' and is a delightful green lane for much of the 3 miles (5 km) north to Litton Cheney Youth Hostel **37** (see top of map on page 81). Allow 50 minutes for the journey to the hostel, heading north, through Park's Dairy Farm, until you reach a T-junction. Turn left and the hostel is about 500 yards away, on the corner opposite the village pub and a small stream.

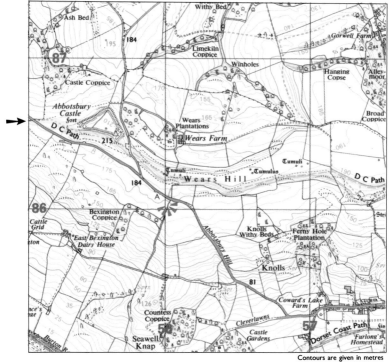

Contours are given in metres
The vertical interval is 5m

The Coast Path itself keeps to the top of the ridge of Wears Hill. At White Hill the ridge broadens. Keep just to the seaward side of the crest of the ridge across a very large field to a corner where the bridleway from Abbotsbury joins the path. Fork left along the fence to the Bishop's Road. Go ahead for 40 yards (35 metres) and turn right through a bridlegate and stay just below a fence at the head of a terraced valley. At the top left hand corner of this wild area the Coast Path crosses a stile and joins a gated farm track. Halfway along there is a prehistoric stone circle. Continue straight on to the southern side of a group of farm buildings.

Cross another road by going a few yards to the north and then strike due east again towards the Hardy Monument **39**.

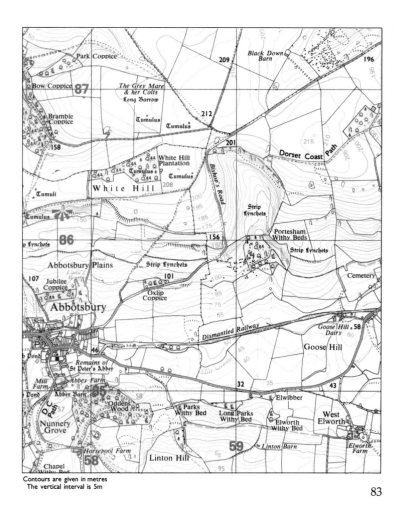

Contours are given in metres
The vertical interval is 5m

The path crosses one field at Portesham Hill and comes to some stone stiles. The Coast Path leads due east for the length of a wall until it comes to Black Down Barn, where it branches north-east through a plantation to the Hardy Monument.

First you may wish to visit the Hell Stone **38**, a reconstructed burial chamber. There is a permissive path which leads diagonally across the field to the south-east from the stone stile. The Hell Stone is a substantial cromlech and although it was reconstructed in the last century there are indications that the present structure strongly resembles the original, which would have been covered by a long mound of earth. (Read more about this on page 90.)

From the Hell Stone continue due north along the wall next to which it stands, and another stone stile brings you back out on the Coast Path, where you turn due east.

The monument **39** is to Admiral Thomas Hardy, of Nelson's flagship at Trafalgar. Hardy was born nearby at Kingston Russell House in 1760 and left to go to sea at the age of 12, although he came back to school at the age of 13 for another

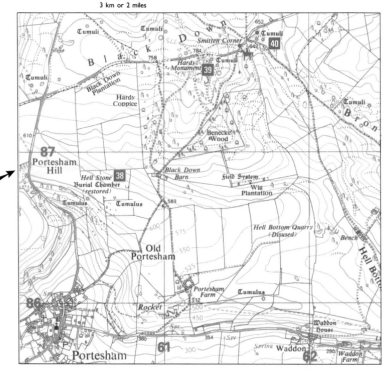

Contours are given in feet
The vertical interval is 25ft

three years. He then took to sea again and in due course joined the Royal Navy, becoming a lieutenant at the age of 21. Two years later he met Nelson and the two worked together until the Battle of Trafalgar in 1805. Hardy subsequently retired to Portesham, just below this monument, and died in 1839 at the age of 79.

The official Coast Path crosses the road opposite the Hardy Monument for a short way to return at Smitten Corner, whence it travels south-eastward down a track beside a group of very distinctive tumuli **40**.

The track stays on the ridge for 3 miles (5 km), and is a bridleway throughout that length. It passes many more tumuli and from it you may make easy diversions to Martinstown

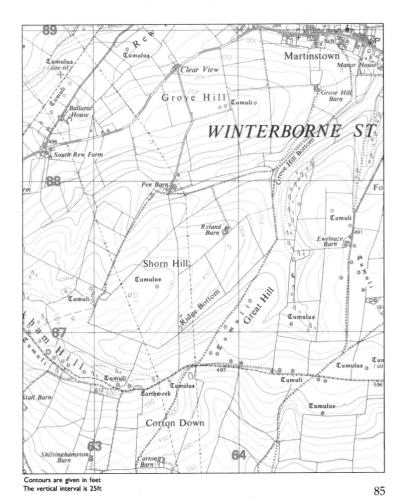

Contours are given in feet
The vertical interval is 25ft

(medieval church), Maiden Castle hill fort **41** and even Dorchester. Further details of the archaeological monuments to be seen along this stretch are on pages 90–1.

After 2½ miles (4 km) along Ridge Hill the path crosses the B3159 Upwey to Martinstown road beside a Weymouth Borough Council marker **42**. It goes straight through the gate opposite and continues along the ridge, which is the Weymouth borough boundary, until it meets at right angles a stony track which is the original route of the Roman road from Dorchester to the port of Weymouth **43**.

The path goes towards Weymouth for 400 yards along this track before turning across a long narrow field to cross the busy A354 Dorchester to Weymouth Road. There it becomes a bridleway once again and runs due east from the Weymouth road, passing north of the entrance of a tunnel on the Weymouth to Dorchester railway.

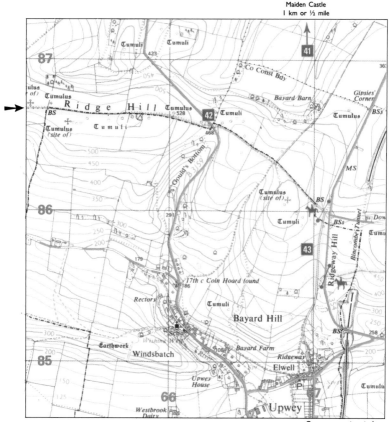

Contours are given in feet
The vertical interval is 25ft

Rejoin the road for a short distance beside the golf course until you reach the next junction. Turn due south down the bridleway opposite the road from Dorchester and follow it down into the village of Bincombe, where you will see the church **44** ahead. Pass to the north of the church and keep on up the farm track. This is clearly waymarked through a number of fields giving good views of strip lynchets, the field systems of medieval farming **45**.

Carry straight on until you come to the top of a steep slope. The official route of the path bears north-east to Greenhill Barton, a group of isolated barns, but an alternative route drops straight down to a stile and proceeds round the seaward side of a small knoll to rejoin the bridleway along West Hill. To the south of this is the hill fort of Chalbury **46**.

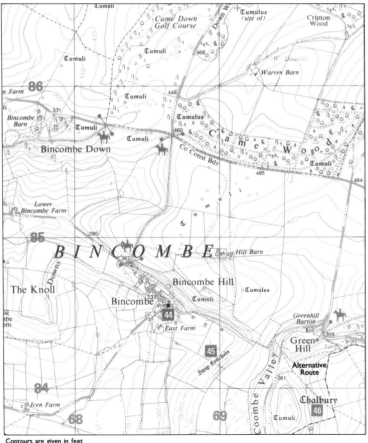

Contours are given in feet
The vertical interval is 25ft

The path follows the bridleway for a further 1¼ miles (2 km), keeping more or less to the top of the steep slope of the ridge overlooking Sutton Poyntz. You pass a number of tumuli **47** to the landward side of the path and reach Northdown Barn, which is ruined, then follow the chalk tracks which lead eastward to White Horse Hill. The Coast Path passes along the northern edge of a large field which stands on top of the hill immediately above the White Horse **48**.

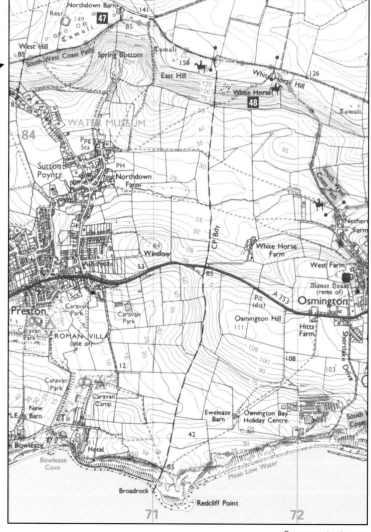

Contours are given in metres
The vertical interval is 5m

The White Horse, cut in the turf on the hills behind Osmington, has George III riding it and was dug in the hillside to commemorate his many visits at the end of the 18th century.

At the eastern end of this large field there is a gateway which comes out to a junction of four bridleways. The Coast Path takes the bridleway leading down the steeper slope to the south-east, which is a rugged farm track leading down between hedges to the village of Osmington.

Find your way to the south-east corner of Osmington, opposite the Sunray Inn. Then walk about 120 yards eastwards along the main road. About 25 yards past the entrance to Craigs Farm Dairy is a footbridge which gives access to the path which then follows a hedgerow all the way to the settlement of Osmington Mills. Walk down the road to the Smuggler's Inn **49** and you are back on the coastal route of the Coast Path.

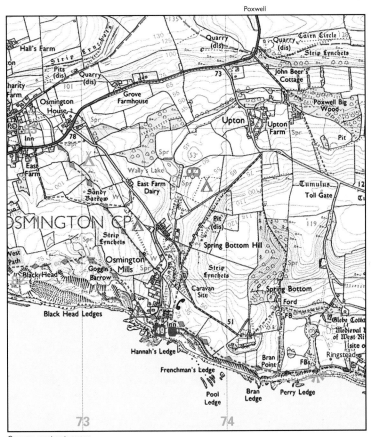

Contours are given in metres
The vertical interval is 5m

Ancient rites on the Dorset and East Devon coasts

At nearly every point on this Coast Path you will be within sight of some evidence of prehistoric occupation.

The long barrows

One of the most ancient and rare prehistoric remains you will see are the long barrows. These are the burial mounds of the New Stone Age (Neolithic period), which lasted from 5000 to 2200 BC in Britain.

Excavations have revealed collections of bones and it seems likely that the practice of allowing the bones first to be pecked clean of flesh after death, as still happens in some Far Eastern countries today, was common in Stone Age times. Subsequently they were buried and covered by the mound.

In some cases the mounds had internal chambers. The Hell Stone **38** on Portesham Hill, just west of the Hardy Monument, is a 19th century reconstruction made from the stone of the structure found in position on the site. Note the round barrows dating from the later, Bronze Age grouped around the Hell Stone.

There is another long barrow, not far from the path, on the ridge to the west of White Horse.

The round barrows

Round barrows were constructed later, in the Bronze Age (2200–650 BC) but it is clear they were deliberately placed near the long barrows. The concentration of round barrows along and near the South Dorset Ridgeway is clearly visible from a great distance. During very clear weather the views from the site are still spectacular, and then you can understand why prehistoric people considered this hill top to be of particular significance in their spiritual lives.

By comparing these with similar monuments in other parts of the country such as Wales and Cornwall, and in Brittany, we can deduce that they were normally used for the burial of extremely important people. Clearly, if just anybody had the right to be buried in this way there would be far more mounds and larger numbers of interments would be found in them.

If you look at them carefully you will see a variety of different forms. A 'bowl' barrow is simply a circular mound; a 'bell' barrow has, or once had, a ditch around it; a 'disk' barrow has a much lower mound, and a ditch which in turn is surrounded by

The Hell Stone burial chamber, a 19th century reconstruction of a prehistoric barrow.

a bank; and the last type is called the 'pond' barrow and is just a hollow surrounded by a bank. Sometimes subsequent ploughing has altered the appearance, but careful archaeological excavation often reveals the original forms.

Along the South Dorset Ridgeway you will see one of the greatest concentrations of round barrows in the British Isles, with nearly 200 on the Ridgeway itself and a further 200 within a very short distance. Allowing for destruction over the ages, both natural and man-induced, there may originally have been more than 1,000 of them. Clearly, 4,000 years ago this part of England had a very special importance for the inhabitants of quite a large area.

Virtually all the mounds that you will see as you follow the Coast Path from Exmouth to Studland can be assumed to be evidence of a Bronze Age civilisation whose lifestyle can be reconstructed by careful observation of the objects which have been found in them during archaeological excavations. In the text I have referred to them loosely as 'tumuli'.

The prehistoric hill fort of Maiden Castle, less than 2 miles from the Ridgeway

section of the Coast Path.

Chesil Beach (or Bank) with the Isle of Portland shimmering in the distance.

8 West Bexington to Osmington Mills via Weymouth

past Abbotsbury and Langton Herring
22½ miles (36.25 km)

The Weymouth route of the Coast Path leaves West Bexington car park by following a track along the back of the Chesil Beach (Chesil Bank) and continues behind the beach for some 2 miles (3 km). After Labour-in-Vain Farm, so called because the land needed much work for little return, the path passes the old coastguard houses and Lawrence's Cottage. Soon you come to more cottages and for about 600 yards the track becomes a surfaced road which soon branches northwards and inland.

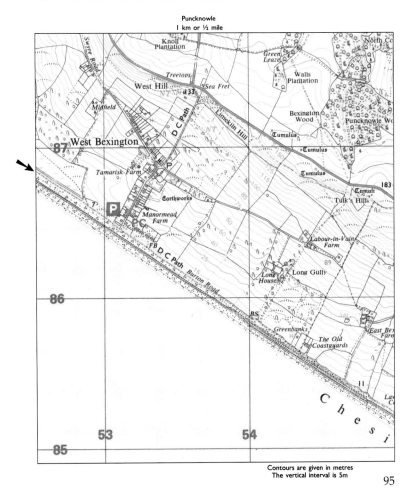

Contours are given in metres
The vertical interval is 5m

This road leads to the Abbotsbury Sub-Tropical Gardens **50**, which are open every day except Christmas Day, Boxing Day and New Year's Day and are well worth a visit. Refreshments are available inside.

The Coast Path continues along the beach for a further 200 yards and then branches inland, curving round to go almost due north-east. Above the path to the north-east is Chapel Hill with the 15th century chapel of St Catherine **51** at its summit.

If you are anxious to make progress eastward, follow the signs along the southern slopes of Chapel Hill, thus avoiding Abbotsbury. Having passed to the seaward side of Chapel Hill, the official route turns due north through the eastern edge of a small copse below the strip lynchets of the hill and behind the old mill. At the northern end of the miller's garden it crosses a small stream and turns south, crosses a stone stile and continues seawards to the Swannery car park.

A second permissive path diverges just north of the Chapel Withy Bed as a shortcut leading straight into the Swannery car park, near the medieval Abbot's Swannery **52**, which is also open to the public.

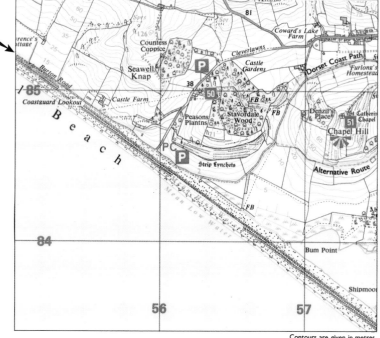

Contours are given in metres
The vertical interval is 5m

There is an hourly mid-summer bus service between Abbotsbury and Weymouth.

If, however, you wish to explore the ruins of the abbey, see one of the largest tithe barns in England **53**, and visit the rather beautiful village of Abbotsbury (see page 74), then detour north to the village.

Whichever way you have chosen to go through Abbotsbury, follow the signs away from the village to the Swannery car park, then follow the road a little way eastward and leave it at Horsepool farm buildings **54**. The route immediately strikes steeply up to the top of the ridge to the east. At the summit of the slope cross a stile and follow the upper side of a fence to the east.

Pass above Clayhanger Farm, behind which there are stiles to negotiate, and keep straight on along the ridge until a well-signed junction indicates where the path drops straight down the slope and to the eastern side of Hodder's Coppice.

At the southern edge of Hodder's Coppice the path crosses another stile to turn once again due east along the south of Ansty's Withy Bed, another small wood. Now cross a small road

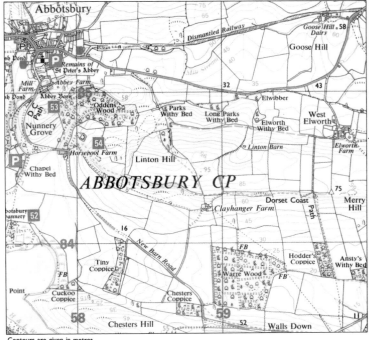

Contours are given in metres
The vertical interval is 5m

at right angles and keep due east, staying parallel to the inland (northern) edge of Wyke Wood. Follow the edge of the wood, turning seawards round its eastern edge, and you will soon come into a valley which leads down to the River Fleet.

You will see a group of buildings straight ahead. Make to the east of these buildings and follow the waymarks parallel to the stream, which is crossed by a small footbridge 300 yards back from the Fleet.

With the minor exceptions mentioned below, the route between this point, Langton Hive and Weymouth stays very close to the shoreline. At Langton Hive Point you will see a small landing stage below former coastguard cottages and a bridleway which leads inland to Langton Herring and the Elm Tree pub.

The Coast Path continues close to the Fleet round a small cove, alongside a long stone wall and over a stile. After a short distance scrambling along grassy banks you come to Fleet House, now known after Falkner's novel as the Moonfleet Hotel, where refreshments may be obtained during opening hours **55**.

It is a half-hour walk along the Coast Path between the Moonfleet Hotel and the old Fleet Church at Butterstreet, where

Boats beside the Fleet.

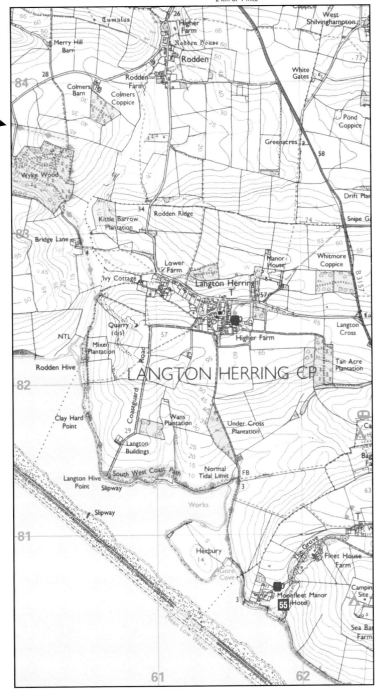

Contours are given in metres
The vertical interval is 5m

only the chancel remains after the rest of the church was destroyed by waves during a tempest in 1824 when the sea broke through the Chesil Bank. In the exciting *Moonfleet* story this is where the smugglers' kegs were hidden in the vaults.

The route crosses the small creek below the church, passes to the seaward side of a camping site at East Fleet Farm and close to a landing stage with a small group of fishermen's huts at Chickerell Hive Point. Just east of this and to the landward side of the path are the army huts of Chickerell Camp.

Shortly after this you will come to the Chickerell rifle range at Tidmoor Point **56**. If the red flags are flying, firing is taking place. A sentry should be posted on each side of the range and will direct you along the well waymarked Coast Path diversion.

If the red flags are not flying and no firing is taking place the official route of the Coast Path keeps to the top of the low cliff around the firing range.

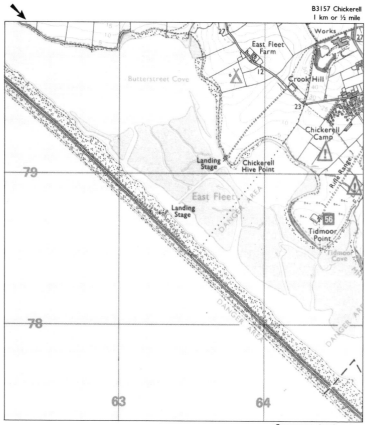

Contours are given in metres
The vertical interval is 5m

On the eastern side of the rifle range cross a footbridge and a little further on enter the Littlesea Holiday Park, passing to the seaward side of all the caravans and still keeping close to the Fleet. At the southern end of the camp site the Coast Path enters an attractive, overgrown area and emerges from this into an open meadow.

Another military installation, the Royal Engineers Bridging Camp **57**, now has to be passed to the landward side. The army has provided a fenced footpath all the way round the outside of the camp. This joins the access road to the camp at its entrance, and between the main entrance to the camp and the edge of the Fleet the Coast Path follows this road.

From the bridging camp to Ferry Bridge the path follows the Fleet through open fields bordered on the far side by the suburb of Wyke Regis, Weymouth, until it eventually reaches the Chesil Beach Holiday Centre. Keep to the seaward side of as many

Contours are given in metres
The vertical interval is 5m

caravans as you can and follow the signs to the main road. Some 500–600 yards (450–550 metres) along the causeway to Portland is the Ferry Bridge Centre where excellent displays explain all about the birds and ecology of the Fleet.

If you have time, the clifftop walks of Portland offer superb views. You could join a guided walk, and there is also a fascinating museum to visit.

From Ferry Bridge to Weymouth Harbour is an easy walk of some 2 miles (3 km).

At Ferry Bridge follow the small concrete path for a short distance and then follow the shores of Portland Harbour, between the sea and a disused railway line, as far as the Weymouth Windsurfing School, where the official path goes behind the building. Continue to Old Castle Road, which leads to Sandsfoot Castle **58**. Henry VIII's Sandsfoot Castle was built in 1539, when an invasion was feared, and it is said that fragments of medieval stonework in its walls were brought from Bindon Abbey at Wool.

Follow Old Castle Road for a short distance more, and then continue along the path which still follows the shores of Portland Harbour and connects Sandsfoot with the Nothe Gardens. At the far end of these is the Nothe Fort **59**, built to counter the Napoleonic threat and now open to the public, with displays on its role in maritime defence. The nearby ferry crosses the harbour for a small fee. Weymouth harbour is quite attractive – fishing boats are often tied up to the quay beside the ferries. There are several harbourside pubs and a museum devoted to shipwrecks and diving, which is worth a visit.

It was George III who started the fashion for Weymouth as a seaside resort. He came year after year. The town was so grateful that a statue to him was erected at the western end of the sea front. If you look to the east you may be able to see the chalk figure of George III on horseback cut in the hillside.

Make now for the Esplanade of Weymouth, one of the finest 18th century seaside façades of any resort in England, although in the summer it can be rather noisy and crowded.

If you are starting or finishing your journey at this point there are hourly trains from Weymouth to London (three hours) and a two-hourly service to Bristol, Cardiff and points beyond via Yeovil. In addition there are daily fast direct services by train to all parts of the country via Poole. There are also daily connections to all areas of the country by coach, and ferry services to the Channel Islands.

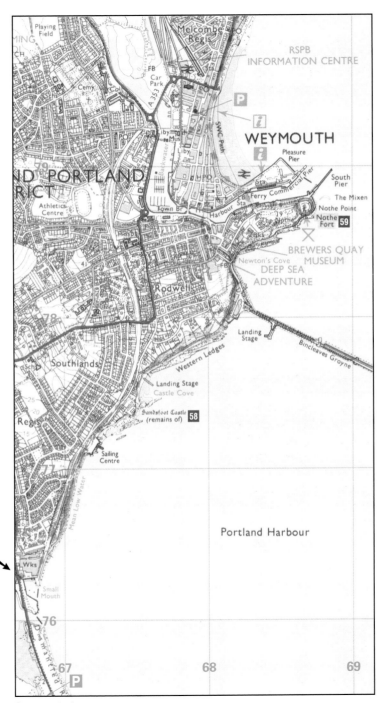

Contours are given in metres
The vertical interval is 5m

To continue east from Weymouth follow the sea wall in front of Lodmoor, the lagoons on the landward side are the site of an RSPB reserve. At the eastern end of the sea wall, the path follows the road and grassy areas beside it heading east, and there are signs to the remains of the Roman temple of Jordan Hill. Follow the sea wall to Overcombe Corner and then onwards to Bowleaze Cove.

The path then passes to the northward side of the Riviera Hotel, coming quite quickly to Redcliff Point. From Redcliff Point to the holiday centre **60** is three-quarters of a mile (1200 metres) and the path remains near the cliff all the way.

Two-thirds of a mile (1 km) east of the holiday camp, and after passing Black Head, look out for a stile across a fence on the landward side of the clifftop field above Osmington Mills (see map on page 109). Follow a narrow path down to the road. Keep right where the path rejoins the eastern end of the Inland Route, and turn right down the road to the Smugglers Inn.

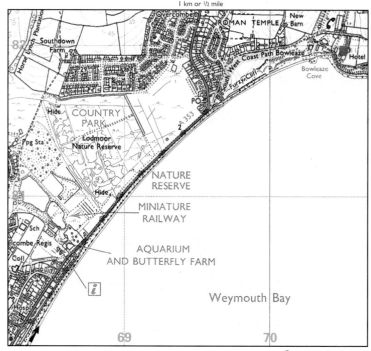

Contours are given in metres
The vertical interval is 5m

The ports of Weymouth Bay

Many of the towns and villages through which the Coast Path passes were important ports before the coming of the railways. It is only during this century that their significance has dwindled, with tourism taking the first place in their economies, although Weymouth and Poole still have ferry services to France and the Channel Islands, as well as freight cargo shipments.

In Roman times Kimmeridge was an industrial centre. No evidence of a Roman quay remains, but various unsuccessful attempts were made through the ages to develop it as a commercial port and traces of the quays can still be found there.

A safer haven and natural miniature harbour was at Lulworth Cove, still used for this purpose today.

Portland Harbour was built by convicts between 1849 and 1903.

The harbour at Weymouth must have been used in Roman times since a Roman road, still used, leads from Dorchester, which had straight and direct road links with London.

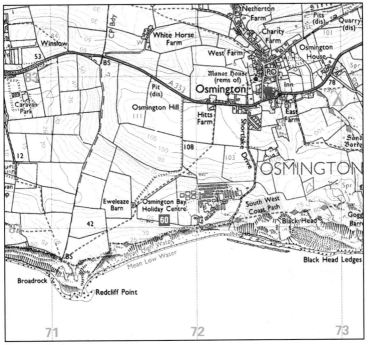

Contours are given in metres
The vertical interval is 5m

Weymouth still has a bustling port with the local fishing industry as well

The port first made news when a ship unloading here brought the Black Death to England in 1348. In medieval times Weymouth on the western side of the River Wey and Melcombe Regis on the eastern were both important ports. There seems to have been some decline in the late medieval period, but both harbours were active again during Elizabethan and Jacobean times.

We must remember that until the coming of the train and efficient road services, one of the best ways of getting to other parts of the country, including London, would have been by boat. The young architect and author Thomas Hardy travelled in this way from London to Dorchester.

Weymouth was also important in maintaining British contacts with the Channel Islands, particularly during times of tension with France, and when we were being friendly towards our neighbours there would have been a lot of trade with Normandy.

as cross-Channel ferries.

The port of Weymouth was in decline when quite suddenly doctors produced a theory that resting by the sea and sea bathing were good for you, thus Melcombe Regis became a fashionable resort. When the railway arrived in 1857, providing a direct link to London via Dorchester and Westbury as well as links to many other parts of the south coast of England via Southampton, the tourist trade was given an enormous boost.

The line that brought Brunel's Great Western Railway to Weymouth from thriving 19th century Bristol and fashionable Bath Spa is still in operation and it is an attractive journey, as you meander through rural Dorset, Somerset and Wiltshire. It was in order to boost trade on this line that the Great Western inaugurated their own Weymouth to Cherbourg service and 11 years later, in 1889, started their London–Weymouth–Channel Islands run, the fastest land-sea route.

The port of Weymouth is also still a haven for fishing boats as well as pleasure boats of all sizes, and it continues to thrive.

9 Osmington Mills to Lulworth Cove

past White Nothe and Durdle Door
6¼ miles (10 km)

The car park at Osmington Mills belongs to the Smugglers Inn and is primarily for the use of customers during opening hours, although the publican has no objection to customers going for a walk between times.

Going east, proceed nearly to the front door of the pub and then skirt round the landward side of the bars, by the old wooden coastguard cottages. After crossing one stile the Coast Path goes to the top, seaward side of the first field, and crosses another stile, and then keeps to the cliff top for a further 1¼ miles (2 km).

Just to the east of the modern settlement of Ringstead **61** there is a field beside the Coast Path, enclosed on all sides by woods. This is the site of the deserted medieval village of Ringstead.

Osmington and Ringstead from White Nothe.

Local legend has it that French pirates burnt the village to the ground, killed all the men and carried off the women and children.

It is, however, more likely that such villages were deserted partly because of the Black Death, or, even more mundanely and commonly, because of economic and agricultural changes that destroyed the livelihood of the inhabitants. Records for Ringstead, however, show that the actual population change of the area was minimal, and so the desertion of the village may be better explained by the dispersion of the population as they went to live in places more convenient to their work, scattered around the immediate locality. When the grass is short and the weather dry, the traces of the village street and the cottages can still be seen.

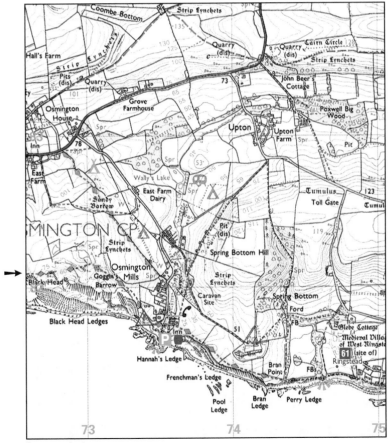

Contours are given in metres
The vertical interval is 5m

At the new settlement of Ringstead, the Coast Path goes inland for a little way and then strikes eastward along a track to the seaward side of the car park. The track passes a small caravan site and goes through an area of thicket.

The Coast Path emerges after the thicket on to a lawn beside Burning Cliff, so called because it ignited spontaneously in the 19th century and became a popular tourist attraction. The undercliff here is National Trust land and a narrow path gives access to the beach at this point **62**.

Meanwhile the Coast Path follows a track east, to the landward side of the chapel of St Catherine, and keeps straight on where the track bears inland, beside a bungalow, before emerging at the gates of Holworth House.

Between this point and Durdle Door it is 3 miles (5 km) and the route stays on the cliff top throughout.

From the former coastguard cottages at White Nothe **63** there are superb views of the nature reserve, and a precipitous path

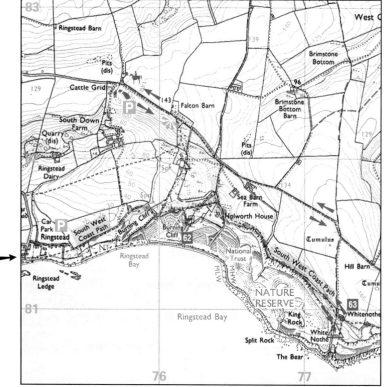

Contours are given in metres
The vertical interval is 5m

leads westward under King Rock and back down to the beach. It is easier and safer, however, to find your way from the bottom rather than the top, and if you have descended to the beach at the western end you may like to rejoin the Coast Path by this route. It is, however, a climb that should be avoided by those who suffer from vertigo.

From White Nothe the Coast Path keeps to the cliff edge except to skirt around the back of West Bottom. There will be no problems in either direction, and this is one of the quieter parts of the Coast Path.

Looking south you see the Isle of Portland across Weymouth Bay. The clifftop walks of Portland itself offer superb views and if you have a chance to go on one of the guided walks there or visit the museum you should take the opportunity, the history of the 'Island' is fascinating.

Looking east the first distinctive feature is Bat's Head: a triangular cliff jutting out of the sea with a narrow cave going through it. Beyond that is Durdle Door and the high ground of Hambury Tout, followed by the Lulworth army ranges.

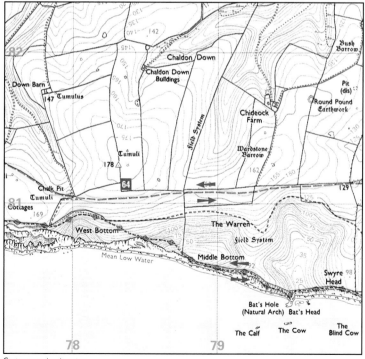

Contours are given in metres
The vertical interval is 5m

The path drops steeply into a small valley called Scratchy Bottom, just west of Durdle Door, a limestone archway pierced over the years by the waves to make it one of the most famous landmarks on the south coast of England. The name 'Durdle' comes from the Saxon *durch* meaning 'through' and 'Door' is the more modern equivalent to signify the opening in the rock.

There is a track leading up to the nearby car park and caravan site where there are toilets, telephones and refreshments. Meanwhile, heading east, the Coast Path stays on top of the cliff, rising to Hambury Tout. Below there are dramatic chalk cliffs of many colours with Durdle Door in the near distance, Bat's Head with its small cave in the middle distance and White Nothe, Weymouth Bay and Portland completing the scene.

At this point Lulworth Cove and the Lulworth army ranges come into sight. The official route of the Coast Path currently follows the fence line by the cliff and the houses at Stair Hole, but most walkers will wish to carry straight on down through the car park and into the main village street of Lulworth Cove. A summer bus service sometimes operates to Wool station.

(For those going west, simply cross the Lulworth Cove car park on this track and keep to the cliff path all the way to Weymouth.)

At Lulworth Cove it is worth exploring Stair Hole with its caves pierced through the limestone mass, allowing the sea to wash out the softer clays behind. This may be what Lulworth Cove looked like millions of years ago, before the sea penetrated as far as the chalk cliffs of Bindon Hill behind. From Stair Hole one has a superb view of the Lulworth Crumple, which illustrates the geological folding that gives this area such an unusual and varied landscape. Lulworth Cove itself has full facilities including refreshments.

Just inland at East Lulworth is the 17th century ruin of Lulworth Castle. In the grounds is a church with a 15th century tower and font, although the remainder was restored in the last century. The family who owned the castle were friendly with George III and are one of the great old Catholic families of England. It is said that George III gave permission for the construction of a Catholic church in the grounds of the castle so long as it did not have the appearance of being a church.

The poet John Keats spent his last days in England at Lulworth, having come ashore while becalmed on his way to Italy, where it was thought his illness might be cured.

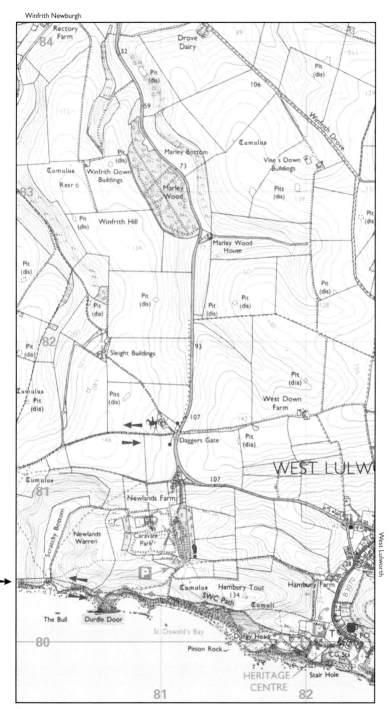

Contours are given in metres
The vertical interval is 5m

113

Pre-Roman times on the coast

On virtually every day while walking along this Coast Path you will see at least one prehistoric hill fort. These vary from quite simple enclosures with one bank and ditch around them, as at Branscombe, to the large, impressive establishments with many ditches, as at Maiden Castle, which is Iron Age in origin.

Signs of occupation have been found in a number of the hill forts which have been excavated. They were probably all inhabited and treated as refuges by the surrounding population. The houses discovered in them were round or rectangular and reconstructions of how they may have looked in Iron Age times can be seen at the Butser Ancient Farm in Hampshire. No ponds or wells have ever been found in these hilltop forts. We assume that maximum use was made of any rainwater that fell on the area or that people descended to the nearest stream.

We can be fairly sure that the hill forts were important centres, but we may never know how far their jurisdiction extended. Recent archaeological finds show that there were also lowland farms at this time, but these are not visible in the way that the hilltop enclosures are. The earliest inhabitants of the area were purely hunters and gatherers of fruit and other plant products. The only traces they have left are their stone implements which you can view in the excellent local museums.

Gradually, Neolithic people incorporated farming into their activities. Some of this would leave no trace, but as time went on enclosures would have been necessary to contain livestock and mark boundaries between fields.

The archway of Durdle Door, created by the action of waves beating against the limestone.

The associated patterns you will see on hill sides from time to time, if you are lucky enough to catch them in the right light, are the so-called 'Celtic' field systems. They show best where the vegetation is short or during droughts, and the best time to see them is in early morning and late evening.

The fields associated with prehistoric farming are not the broad level terraces which you will see alongside the Coast Path, particularly in Dorset. These terraces are medieval in origin, although they may overlie the 'Celtic' fields.

If you identify a criss-cross pattern of squares and rectangles much smaller than modern fields, between one-sixth of an acre and $1\frac{1}{2}$ acres (0.07 to 0.6 hectares), you may be looking at evidence of some of the earliest farming in Britain.

We are fairly certain that such fields were used during the Iron Age, from 650 BC to the coming of the Romans, and it

The cliffs of Swyre Head from Durdle Door.

116

would appear that Dorset farmers continued to use them during the Roman occupation.

We do not know if the changes in customs during prehistoric times were caused by mass migrations of population or by the influence of the successful and powerful neighbours of Britain causing changes by more peaceful means.

We cannot be certain, therefore, whether the coastal hill forts were put up primarily by immigrants protecting themselves from a hostile local population, or whether the local population put them up to defend themselves from foreign invasion. Perhaps both happened at different periods of history.

From archaeological evidence we do know, however, that shortly before the coming of the Romans in A D 43 there were various trading establishments on the south coast of England. Inhabitants of Kent in particular were drinking wine and adopting other Roman fashions some time before the actual invasion took place. Hengistbury Head, a prominent landmark at Christchurch and clearly visible from the eastern end of this path, is known to have been a trading centre with Europe.

It is only with the coming of the Romans and the advent of written history that we can be more certain about what was going on at the time. It would seem that further east in England some of the tribes gave in to the Romans without major resistance.

However, the inhabitants of the area through which this path passes put up a very spirited resistance to the Roman invasion. The 'inland route' of the Coast Path in Dorset passes within walking distance of Britain's most spectacular Iron Age hill fort, Maiden Castle.

At the eastern entrance to this hill fort archaeologists have found evidence of a major battle. Most of the finds are well displayed and explained in the Dorset County Museum at Dorchester, and Maiden Castle is well worth a detour. At the complex eastern entrance, piles of sling stones from the Chesil Beach were found, as well as remains of the dead Britons massacred here. One of the bodies had a Roman ballista lodged through his spine.

We can conclude from this that the British defenders were not skilled in archery and relied on sling stones in their unsuccessful attempt to resist the efficient and well-armed Romans.

If you want to know more about this period I can thoroughly recommend museums in the towns through which you pass, as well as the Dorset County Museum.

10 Fossil forest to Broad Bench

around Lulworth Cove and Kimmeridge Bay
$6\frac{3}{4}$ *miles (11 km)*

LULWORTH RANGES WARNING

All visitors to Lulworth Ranges must note that this is an Army Range and the public have no right of access when firing is taking place.

General Instructions.
1. Keep within waymarks on each path. Do not leave these marked paths.
2. Comply with the warden's instructions at all times.
3. Do not touch or pick up any ammunition or any other object you may see.
4. Please do not enter any buildings.
5. Please protect the wildlife. Do not take specimens.
6. Camping or making fires is not permitted.

Range Walk Symbols (maps on pages 124, 125, 126 and 127).

━ ━ ━ ━ ━ ━ Range Walks

🏠   Range Walk starting point

The permissive path 'A' to 'B' through the Lulworth army ranges (as shown on the map on pages 120–1) is normally open to the public most weekends and school holidays. More information on the exact opening times can be obtained by dialling Bindon Abbey (01929) 462721 and asking for the Range Office. When the Coast Path is open, the range walks are also open to the public.

The road from East Lulworth to Steeple, 'C' to 'D', is often open in the evenings and on days when no firing is taking place on that particular part of the Lulworth army ranges. Signboards are posted on roads approaching the area and will indicate whether this road is open at the time. The road, 'E' to 'F', is also open when no firing is taking place and is often open when all other roads through the ranges are closed. At times when the path, 'A' to 'B', the East Lulworth to Steeple Road, 'C' to 'D', and the East Lulworth to West Holme Road, 'E' to 'F', are all closed, the walker will have to find a way of circumnavigating the whole of this area via Coombe Keynes, East Stoke, East Holme, Stoborough and Steeple.

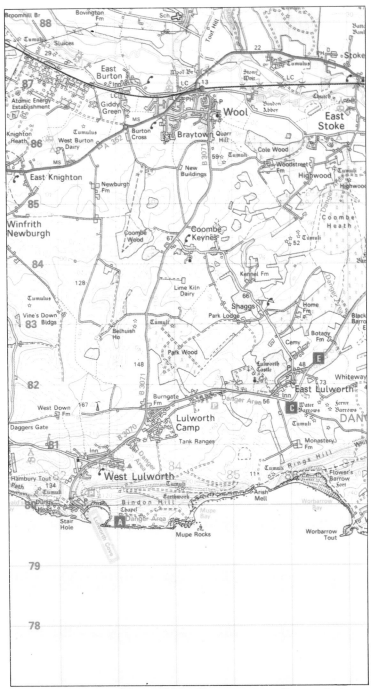

Scale approx 1 inch to 1 mile

Contours are given in metres
The vertical interval is 10m

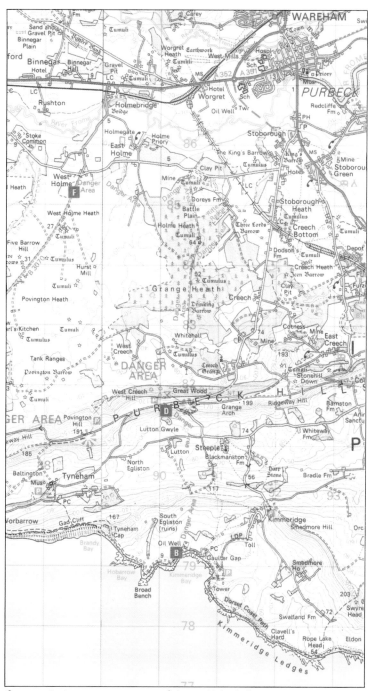

Contours are given in metres
The vertical interval is 10m

Scale approx 1 inch to 1 mile

121

The hard limestone bands of Mupe Rocks resist fierce storms, while the softer

lays and chalk behind are washed away.

If you have planned your visit carefully and the range walks are open, follow the pavement up the road towards Lulworth village and look for a sign right which will take you to the top of the cliffs behind Lulworth Cove. If the tide is low enough you may walk on the beach but there is a danger of falling rocks.

The path descends to Little Bindon **65**, a small cottage once associated with the medieval monastery mentioned on page 76. The access to the Lulworth army ranges is immediately to the east of Little Bindon. Once inside the ranges, follow the boundary to the cliff top where you will see below you the fossil forest **66**.

Do not be disappointed by what you see. The round, bowl-like lumps of rock, some of which are hollow, once contained tree stumps of a forest which grew here perhaps 135 million years ago. The lumps of rock are the remains of the growths which formed round the trees. Further along you can see the ripple marks of an ancient beach.

These are the only fossil remains in this area. The fossil forest is a designated Site of Special Scientific interest and the use of geological hammers in this area is illegal.

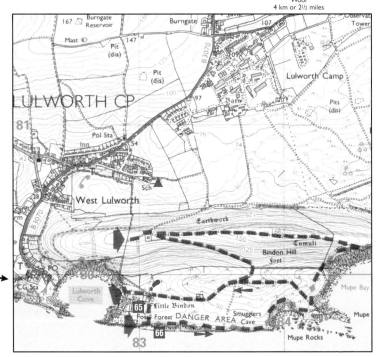

Contours are given in metres
The vertical interval is 5m

From the top of the steps at the fossil forest the Path continues eastwards keeping close to the cliff. It is indicated by yellow posts and the area so marked has been cleared of all explosive materials. After about 800 yards the path reaches Mupe Rocks and Mupe Bay (see page 128 for a circular walk).

The path between Mupe and Kimmeridge Bays is almost immediately adjacent to the cliff top all the way.

From Mupe Bay there is a stiff climb to the summit of Bindon Hill. From here on the going is arduous and there is no way out for another 3 miles (5 km). The views are magnificent and the scenery most unusual since it has not been intensively farmed for more than 70 years. Looking southwards, the view is of Mupe Rocks, the limestone remains which protect the softer chalks behind from erosion. The cliffs immediately below are of pure chalk and views to the east are of Worbarrow Tout. In the cliffs of the bay you can see the many coloured clays which lie between the limestone and the chalk in this area.

Now comes Arish Mell, a small shingle beach with chalk cliffs. There is no public access to the beach, which has not been cleared of explosives. The path rises again steeply to the top of

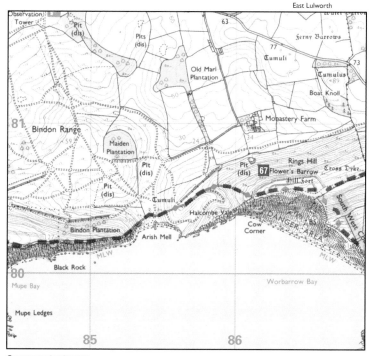

Rings Hill where there are the remains of an Iron Age hill fort called Flower's Barrow **67**. From here the path descends very steeply at first to Worbarrow Bay, until 1943 a small fishing settlement.

Worbarrow Beach is open to the public when the range walks are open and it is safe for bathing. You can clamber up to the top of Worbarrow Tout for wonderful views of the surroundings. Just to the east of Worbarrow Tout is Pondfield with its fascinating marine wildlife.

For more information about the marine life call in at the Dorset Wildlife Trust's Information Centre at Kimmeridge Bay **71**. For details about the history and natural history of the Tyneham valley, visit the information centre in Tyneham Church **68**. The old Tyneham village schoolroom has been restored to its 1920's layout and furnishing and gives a fascinating insight into those times.

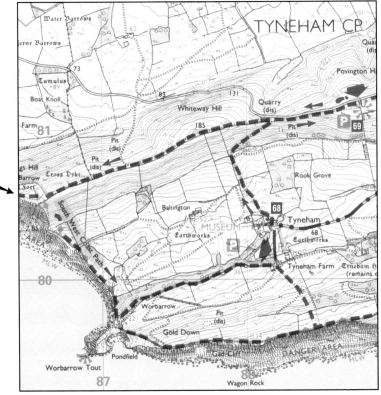

Contours are given in metres
The vertical interval is 5m

If you strike inland from Worbarrow along the well-frequented track beside the stream and woods to visit Tyneham, you may return to the Coast Path directly at the top of Gad Cliff by a path which leads southward from the village car park. If you need to press on eastwards, climb over the stile beside Worbarrow Tout for a steep climb on to Gold Down and Gad Cliff.

Halfway along Gad Cliff you will pass the junction which leads down to Tyneham village and then you will come to another junction where the Coast Path user must be careful to turn south-east towards Kimmeridge Bay for the descent. First of all this zigzags down the slopes of Tyneham Cap, and then it rejoins the cliff edge, coming only slightly inland to take the short-cut across the headland of Broad Bench. The path then continues along the low black cliffs off Kimmeridge all the way to the Kimmeridge oil well **70**, which has been in production since 1957.

You are now outside the army ranges.

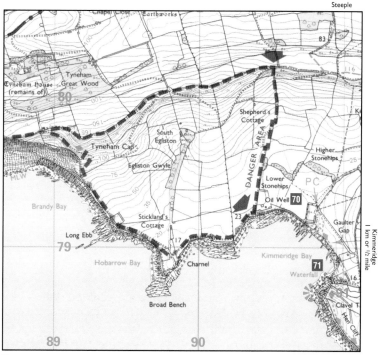

Contours are given in metres
The vertical interval is 5m

A CIRCULAR WALK BETWEEN LULWORTH COVE AND MUPE ROCKS
3 miles (4.8 km) (see map on page 124)
(see page 119 for details about Lulworth ranges and firing times)

Follow the path from Lulworth Cove to Mupe Rocks (see pages 124 and 125). Those who do not wish to continue through the ranges from Mupe Bay can return to Lulworth Cove by following the jeep track all the way back, directly to Little Bindon. Alternatively, turn inland along another jeep track which rises towards the radar station. This will enable you to leave the army ranges immediately west of the radar station and descend to West Lulworth village and its youth hostel, which are signed from that point.

Tyneham

Visits to Tyneham may only take place during Lulworth Range opening times – that is most weekends and school holidays. It is dangerous to enter the area at any other time. If in doubt, ring Bindon Abbey (0929) 462721 for opening times.

To walk to Tyneham start from the Whiteway Hill car park and picnic area **69** on the ridge overlooking Tyneham. Go through the wicket gate west and carry on straight along the ridge, keeping between the yellow painted posts which define the area that has been cleared of explosives. Keep going until you reach the cliff top at Rings Hill where you will find the massive embankments of Flower's Burrow, an Iron Age hill fort contemporary with many others along this coastline **67**. It is not certain whether this hill fort originally had ramparts on the seaward side; these may have been washed away in the succeeding 2,000 years. You can read more about these forts on page 114.

This first part of the walk is extremely easy, flat walking on short turf. The elderly or infirm should retrace their steps from the hill fort, having enjoyed outstanding views over the Tyneham Valley and towards St Aldhelm's Head in the east and the Isle of Portland in the west.

The next part of the walk calls for good walking shoes and caution, as it descends steep banks which can be very slippery.

Descend the Coast Path east until you come to Worbarrow Bay. Ahead is Worbarrow Tout. The beach is safe for bathing and open during range walk opening times. From Worbarrow Tout turn inland up the Tyneham Valley along a flint track. One mile inland the track turns sharply to the left into Tyneham car park and the deserted village of Tyneham.

In the church **68** there is a display explaining the geology and prehistory of the area, and its history from the medieval occupation of the valley to the handing over of the area to the army in 1943. Leaflets are also on sale explaining many of the features of interest along the Dorset Heritage Coast.

Note also the expertly restored memorial to the Williams family in the north transept, the 13th century piscina, the small and simple memorial to Elizabeth Tarrant on the north wall of the nave, and the Martin Travers window of the mother and child under a growing tree above the altar.

Just opposite the church is the old village schoolroom. This was in use until 1932 and all children of school age attended the same school, with a small platform at the eastern end being reserved for the infants. In the schoolroom there is now an exhibition about the school in the 1920's.

The wildlife of the Lulworth army ranges is unique because many parts of the area have never been affected by agricultural practices, which have changed the scenery so much elsewhere over the past 40 years.

Coming out of the schoolroom go to the right of the church through a gateway which leads to another steep track up to the top of the ridge, where you turn right for the Whiteway Hill car park **69**.

Marine wildlife on the coast of Dorset and East Devon

While walking the Coast Path it is worth sparing some time to take a well-earned breather and explore the sea shore along this coast which exhibits excellent examples of most marine habitats.

The Dorset coast between Swanage and Weymouth provides the walker with the opportunity to experience the lower part of the shore, exposed for long periods on spring tides (following a new or full moon), owing to the rare phenomenon of a double low tide which affects this area.

The keen-eyed Coast Path walker may notice that some species occur in abundance on Devon and West Dorset shores but are not found further east. The explanation is that such species, sea urchins are an example, are southern creatures

The deserted village of Tyneham, taken over by the army in 1943.

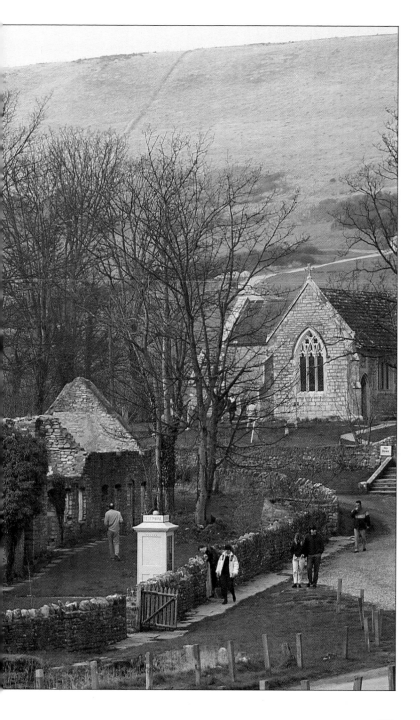

associated with the Gulf Stream. The Dorset Wildlife Trust's Purbeck Marine Wildlife Reserve, the first of many in Britain, contains several seaweeds and animals which are at their easternmost limit in the Channel. Look out for the spectacular iridescent seaweed *Cystoseira tamariscifolia*, blue, purple or turquoise.

The aims of the reserve, which relies on voluntary co-operation, are to promote quiet enjoyment of the marine environment and to educate visitors about marine wildlife and its conservation. At Kimmeridge Bay, the main access point to the reserve, the reserve warden is on hand to show visitors the varied marine life and lead guided seashore walks. The Dorset Trust's information centre **71** (next to the slipway) contains a wildlife display and a rock pool aquarium.

At Kimmeridge you will see divers setting out in their inflatable boats to dive on the ledges and wrecks in the area or to explore the Purbeck Marine Wildlife Reserve's underwater nature trail in Worbarrow Bay. The rocky ledges provide horizontal and vertical surfaces for plants and plant-like animals to colonise, and cracks and crevices for crabs, lobsters and fish to hide in. Wrecks are like artificial reefs and rich in wildlife.

Kimmeridge Bay is an excellent rocky shore to explore because of its clear water, rock pools and carpet of colourful seaweeds: bright green sea lettuce contrasts with the pink coralline weed and the hold-fasts (anchors) of the large strap-like kelps provide a refuge for many tiny animals – sea squirts, sea mats and brightly striped blue-rayed limpets. Beadlet and snakelocks anemones, bright yellow periwinkles, crabs and shrimps make up this rock pool world.

Other good rocky shores, well worth a detour, are Osmington Mills, Eype Mouth and the ledge between Charmouth and Lyme Regis. Check the tides before venturing out on to these ledges.

At first glance sandy shores, such as Studland and Charmouth, appear barren compared with rocky ones. On closer inspection, however, you can spot the signs of the animals which live buried in the sand: lugworm casts, sand-mason tubes, meticulously built out of sand grains and shell fragments, empty shells and if you are lucky a masked crab, superbly camouflaged, hiding just beneath the sand surface.

Sand dunes consist of wind-blown sand trapped and stabilised by various hardy plants, such as the coarse marram grass. Older dune systems provide conditions in which a wide variety of plants, such as heathers, can grow.

The mud-flats and salt-marsh areas of the sheltered shores of Poole Harbour, the Fleet and the Axe, Otter and Exe estuaries provide feeding grounds and roosting areas for wading birds, such as curlew, dunlin, redshank and oystercatcher, which probe the mud for worms and shellfish, and also grazing areas for ducks and geese. The Fleet, a brackish lagoon, tidal at the eastern end, contains vast beds of eelgrass, a favourite food of Brent geese and swans. The western margins of the Fleet can be visited from the Swannery, Abbotsbury, open in spring and summer.

Shingle is moved and deposited along the shore by waves and currents and is generally too unstable to support marine life. On the Chesil Bank, where the shingle has become stable at the top of the beach, specially adapted plants have colonised: sea pea, sea-kale, sea holly and yellow horned poppy. A section of the Chesil Bank is closed between 1 May and 31 August each year, the nesting season of the terns. There are many coastal and marine events and displays in the area. Contact local tourist information centres for specific information about those that are planned to take place during your visit.

Swans at the Swannery, Abbotsbury.

11 Kimmeridge to Studland

past Worth Matravers and through Swanage
20 miles (33 km)

From the Kimmeridge oil well **70** the path keeps to the cliff top, passes to the seaward side of the row of cottages at Gaulter Gap, and then makes for the Clavel Tower **72** at the eastern end of the Bay. The beach is fascinating for its marine wildlife.

Among the boat houses under the Clavel Tower you find the information centre of the Dorset Wildlife Trust **71**. Entry is free but there is a donations box. The centre is normally open when there are likely to be reasonable numbers of people. Guided walks for the public often start here.

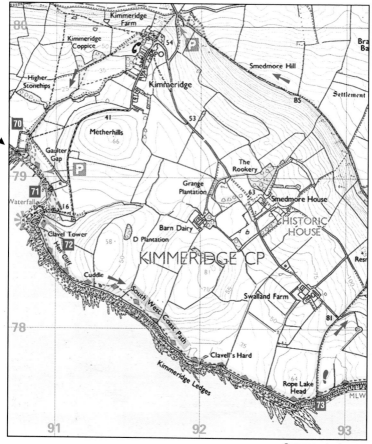

Contours are given in metres
The vertical interval is 5m

From the information centre, retrace your steps a short way up the road and then climb the flight of steps which leads up to the ruined Clavel Tower **72**, built as a folly in the last century and later used as a coastguard look-out. The path now continues along the cliff edge for the next 2 miles (3 km). Beware of crumbling cliffs on the stretch between Clavell's Hard and Egmont Bight.

Between the Clavel Tower and Clavell's Hard, you may see traces of a cutting for the railway which used to take the shale down to a quay below the Clavel Tower.

On the ledges at Clavell's Hard you may be able to pick out the eight holes in the rock which took the posts supporting the small quay used to load barges with shale for export. 'Hard' means a place where boats can land, or a quay.

Next you pass Rope Lake Head **73**. Although this headland looks distinctive from a distance, it is difficult to tell when you are actually walking on it. The next section of the Coast Path remains just outside the field fences for 2 miles (3 km).

The path soon comes to Freshwater Steps **74**. Here there is a curious little headland with a man-made channel along the top of it and a waterfall at the end. The route branches just a few yards to the north to climb out of the Gwyle (the local name for a small valley) and then continues eastwards to rise steeply to the heights of Houns-tout Cliff.

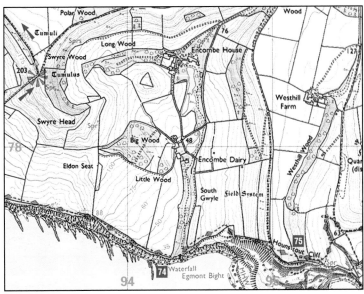

Contours are given in metres
The vertical interval is 5m

Houns-tout **75** is a very distinctive peak, capped with lime-stone, which is porous. This means that water which falls on top of the limestone filters through to the Kimmeridge shales below, which gradually become saturated and turn into a por-ridge-like, semi-fluid mass. From time to time these black layers flow out from under the limestone leaving it without support, and thousands of tons of rock cascade down the cliff and into the sea.

This process has accelerated rapidly in recent years. The path which descended to Chapman's Pool and then rose again the other side has therefore been diverted up the valley to avoid danger. Please follow the signs carefully since the exact route may have been changed to avoid new falls since the time of writing.

The path at the bottom of the steep slope turns left and away from the sea over a stile, through a field, and over a causeway to cross a small stream. Turn right onto a surfaced road which keeps to the level of the contours for about three quarters of a mile (1200 metres). At Hill Bottom Cottage turn right and then right again over a small stream, through an iron bridlegate, and then fork left off the bridleway and up the hill. At the top of the small dry valley turn right on to the plateau of Emmet's Hill (emmet is dialect for ant).

Keep to the cliff top all the way along to Pier Bottom, where there is a dip and rise before you come back on to the top of the plateau to round the corner and come into sight of the Norman chapel of St Aldhelm **76**.

St Aldhelm was a Saxon Bishop of Sherborne, born before the middle of the 7th century. He was educated at Marlborough and Canterbury and later became the Abbot of Marlborough. He founded the monasteries at Frome in Somerset and Brad-ford-on-Avon in Wiltshire. When the diocese of Sherborne was formed, he became its first bishop. Bede wrote about St Aldhelm and commented on his writings. He was reputed to have spoken Latin and Greek as well as being able to read the Bible in Hebrew. He was popular in Wessex because of his use of the vernacular language as he preached to ordinary people.

The term St Alban's, used on the map and by the coastguard, is a misnomer but has gained common currency because the modern tongue finds St Aldhelm's very difficult to pronounce.

The 12th century chapel may also have served at one time as a sea-mark, and the massive Norman vaults and buttress

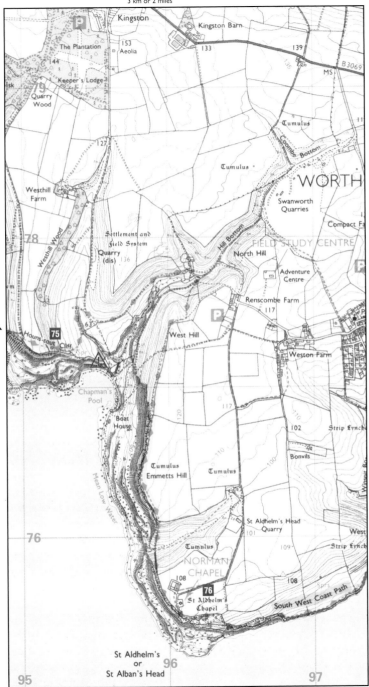

Corfe Castle
3 km or 2 miles

Kingston
Kingston Barn
The Plantation
Aeolia
Keeper's Lodge
Quarry Wood
Westhill Farm
Westhill Wood
Settlement and Field System
Quarry (dis)
Hounstout Cliff
West Hill
Chapman's Pool
Boat House
Mean Low Water
Tumulus
Emmetts Hill
Tumulus
Norman Chapel
St Aldhelm's Chapel
St Aldhelm's or St Alban's Head
Coombe Bottom
WORTH
Swanworth Quarries
Compact Fa
Hill Bottom
North Hill
FIELD STUDY CENTRE
Adventure Centre
Renscombe Farm
Weston Farm
Strip Lynch
Bonvils
St Aldhelm's Head Quarry
West
Strip Lynch
South West Coast Path
B3069

Contours are given in metres
The vertical interval is 5m

137

structures which support it suggest that it once had a more substantial superstructure, which may have carried a light at night to guide sailors on their way.

From St Aldhelm's Head to Swanage there will be few problems. Except for very slight detours inland to descend into hanging valleys at Winspit and Seacombe, the path stays adjacent to the field boundary next to the cliff all the way.

At St Aldhelm's Head you leave behind the magnificent views of Portland, Weymouth Bay, the chalk cliffs of Purbeck and the black cliffs of Kimmeridge shales, and come into view of the Isle of Wight and the solid limestone cliffs of Purbeck.

In the spring the puffins, razorbills and guillemots arrive to nest on the narrow ledges of these cliffs and rear their young, leaving again in late July for a lonely life many miles out to sea. You will also see fulmars, kittiwakes, shags, cormorants and black-backed gulls.

The limestone downland flora and its associated wildlife here are quite outstanding. The National Trust now owns substantial stretches of these cliffs and manages the clifftop meadows in order to protect this flora.

A mile east of St Aldhelm's Head the route turns and goes about 100 yards inland before descending through a thicket to the Winspit Valley. Winspit is a small group of cliff quarries last worked during the Second World War. The old mines can be inspected safely from a distance but do not venture within, because rocks can fall at any time and weigh many tons each.

East of Winspit the path rises behind the quarries and stays on the cliff top until Seacombe. This is a much smaller rocky ledge, and the path detours round the back of the quarries here too.

From the back of the ledges at Seacombe Cliff the path strikes east along the cliff top. There are no problems following the path along this stretch and it soon comes to Headbury Quarry **77**. Looking down you will see one of the cannons from the ship, the *Halsewell*, on its way to India when it was caught in a violent storm and destroyed at Halsewell Bars in 1786. One hundred and sixty-six people died including the captain, his two daughters and two nieces.

The Coast Path continues along the cliff top to Dancing Ledge, with its small swimming pool cut into the rock by quarrymen at the beginning of this century, while a stone sign set in the wall indicates a route north-east to Langton Matravers where there are shops, a post office, pubs and camping sites.

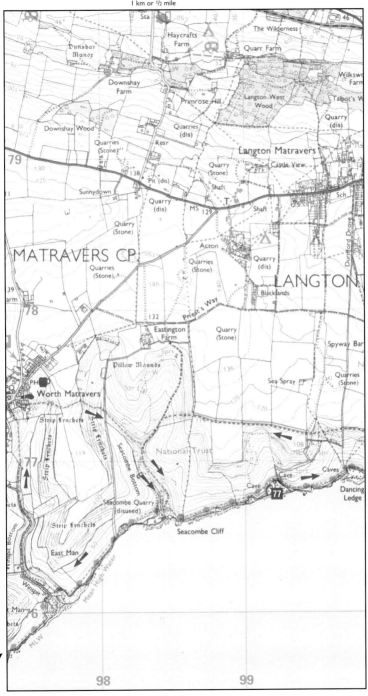

The path soon arrives at the boundary of the National Trust Belle Vue property and then Durlston Country Park, where it stays on the cliff top to Anvil Point lighthouse **78**, built in 1881. Behind the lighthouse there is an excellent Country Park Information Centre **79**. In the Centre you can watch nesting birds live on screen and listen, via a hydrophone, to the dolphins and porpoises travelling up the English Channel. Nearby is Durlston Castle; this was a folly built by Mr Burt, a Swanage man who traded with London and brought many mementoes of London back as ballast after delivering stone. Around Swanage there are frequent reminders of this trade – bollards, the entire façade of the Swanage Town Hall (the Mercer's Hall from London) **80**, a clock tower near the beach **81**, and countless other small items. He also built the castle, installed the enormous globe and had numerous inscriptions carved around the cliff top. Now refreshments may be obtained in the castle, which is licensed.

The path then goes very close to the cliffs, giving superb views in spring of the seabirds below. Follow the cliffs around Durlston Bay through low tamarisk and mature woodland, passing to the seaward side of most of the buildings except where this is impossible. This clifftop route soon emerges on the green areas of Peveril Point and you are now a stone's throw from the centre of Swanage.

(If you are doing the walk east–west, make for Peveril Point coastguard station. Go to the highest corner of the open lawns and follow the signs for Durlston Country Park. After this it is easy to follow the cliffs all the way to St Aldhelm's Head.

Swanage town is worth exploring. The mill pond, the lock-up ('for the punishment of wickedness and vice') behind the town hall **80**, and the Tythe Barn Museum **82** are all worth a visit.

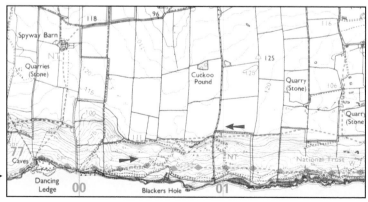

Contours are given in metres
The vertical interval is 5m

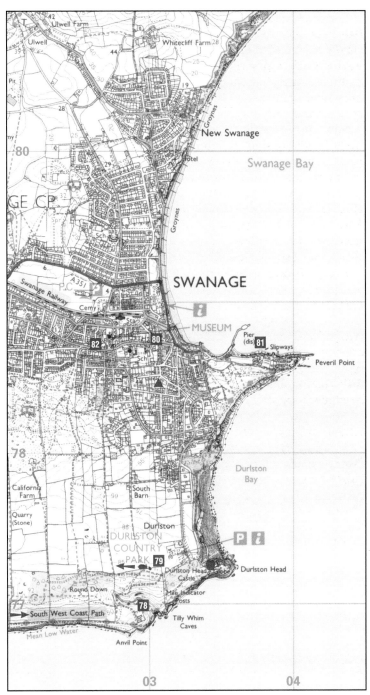

Contours are given in metres
The vertical interval is 5m

141

To get to Studland follow the sea front northwards to the end. Normally you can walk along the beach here to rejoin the path up a small gully at the end of the groynes.

The official Coast Path, however, leaves the Studland road some 800 yards north-west of its junction with the sea front. Waymarks take you back along a private road (public footpath) to the Pines Hotel (refreshments, licensed) and the Ballard Estate. At the northern end of the clifftop lawns follow some steps to cross a small valley where you meet the path from the beach.

The path continues northwards outside the fence to Ballard Point (steep rise) and down to the dramatic white chalk stacks of Old Harry (NT). Keep parallel to the cliff through a coppice and some open fields, soon coming into Studland where there are village shops, car parks, a pub, and access to sandy beaches and the national nature reserve.

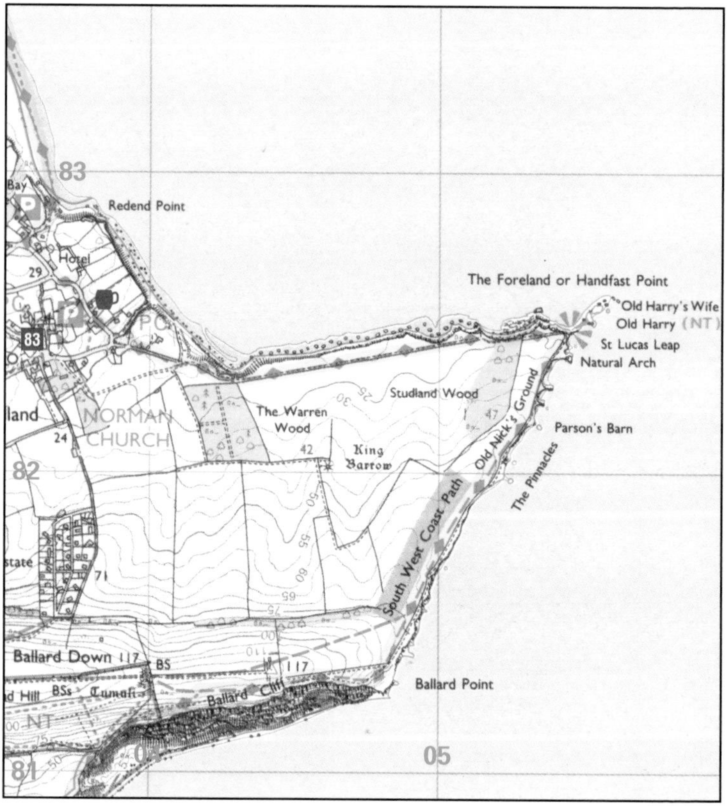

Contours are given in metres
The vertical interval is 5m

The chalk cliffs of the Pinnacles, typical of the spectacular scenery to be found along this coastline.

143

(If you are coming from the opposite direction and have just walked along the beach from the ferry, go as far as you can on the beach and then follow the lane which runs parallel to the sea until it turns sharp right by some toilets. Here you keep straight on along a bridleway and follow the cliffs to Swanage.)

The tiny church of St Nicholas **83** was probably built shortly before the Norman conquest, with the nave being rebuilt in the 11th century, some 12th century alterations, and only minor changes to the structure since that date.

In Studland the path goes along the village lanes until you follow a sign saying Middle Beach car park, where you descend to the beach. From here to South Haven Point **84** is nearly $2\frac{1}{2}$ miles (4 km) of walking on soft sandy beach. It is hard going, although easier near the waterline, and walkers may be forgiven for deciding to take the bus from Studland to South Haven Point which also connects with Poole Station.

From the far side of the chain ferry which takes you to Sandbanks there is another ferry, at hourly intervals in the summer, to Brownsea Island (NT) **85**. There are walks around the island and guided visits to the nature reserve **86** most afternoons.

Little Sea, Studland Heath National Nature Reserve. This Heath is home to many rare species, including all six British reptiles.

Contours are given in metres
The vertical interval is 5m

A CIRCULAR WALK FROM KIMMERIDGE BAY

5 miles (7.8 km) (see maps on pages 134–5)
From Rope Lake Head **73** there is a permissive path, which the local farmer and landowner invite you to use, to get to Swyre Head. Should you wish to return to Kimmeridge from Swyre Head you can follow a bridleway along the top of the ridge, with magnificent views of the surrounding coastal scenery in both directions. The bridleway joins a track, an unsurfaced county road, and you cross the road which leads down to Kimmeridge, to take the path down to Kimmeridge Church. From the church-yard entrance follow the farm track through Kimmeridge Farm and then follow the public footpath, which more or less keeps in the valley parallel with the stream to Gaulter Gap.

A CIRCULAR WALK AT WORTH MATRAVERS

2½ miles (4 km) (see map on page 139)
The village of Worth Matravers has a pub (the Square and Compass) and a post office and two teashops, one with a small museum. The church has a Norman archway and is worth a visit. If you have the chance to take one of the guided walks around the village its fascinating past, including stories of the infamous smuggler Gulliver, as well as the story of Noncon-formist worship in the village blacksmith's, will be revealed.

There is a regular bus service from Swanage to Worth Matravers or there is a car park situated to the north of the village. The bus will leave you on the village green but, from the car park, make your way seaward, leaving the Square and Compass Inn to your left, and you will come into sight of the village green. From the green make your way towards the coast by following the signs for Seacombe next to the bus stop. Go a few yards down a small track giving access to houses, and then turn left along a very narrow path between houses, emerging into a field full of 'strip lynchets' – these were the fields of medieval England.

Go straight across the valley and cross the stone wall by the stile. Keep straight on across the fields until you drop into the Seacombe Valley and then follow the stream down to the sea. To return, turn right (west) at the end of the valley and after three-quarters of a mile the Coast Path brings you to the quarries and rock ledges of Winspit. Turn inland, keeping right at the junction by the treatment works, and you will arrive back at the village green.

Medieval field patterns at Worth Matravers.

A CIRCULAR WALK AT DURLSTON

6¾ miles (10.8 km) (see maps on pages 139–41)

If you are based at Swanage you can walk an upper path from the information centre at Durlston Country Park **79**, returning via the Coast Path.

From the information centre, cross Round Down, keeping to the higher part of the ridge above the 'weirs', the local name for the steep slopes leading down to the sea. A public footpath then follows along the top of the weirs all the way to Dancing Ledge.

To the west of that point the National Trust and a private landowner allow the public to use a continuation which is clearly signed and leads all the way along the top of the steeper slopes to Seacombe Valley. Descend the Seacombe Valley and return by the Coast Path to Durlston Head and Swanage.

Local stone was used to build the houses at Worth Matravers.

Coastal mining and quarrying

The Coast Path between Exmouth and Poole passes countless quarries. Many of the small quarries were for the extraction of chalk and limestone which fed the many lime kilns along the route. If you do the circular walk at Branscombe you will also have seen the copper ore (malachite) quarries above Street, and at Beer you may visit the chalk quarries which produced building stone from the very hard chalk layers there.

One village which is particularly beautiful because of the use of local stone is Abbotsbury. Here the limestone has a large iron content and is therefore a beautiful golden yellow.

The villages which lie to the south of the ridgeway route behind Weymouth are built of a light grey limestone, 'Ridgeway stone', and many of the churches and smaller manor houses of South Dorset are also built from this material. The coastal villages all the way along are built of stone which would have been quarried locally from the nearest hillside but rarely, if ever, exported.

Stone for the cathedrals and cities of England

The exception to this generalisation comes at Portland and Purbeck. Here the building stone has been exported since Roman times. The ready access to convenient transport by sea meant that the stone was easy to export, and it can be seen in medieval cathedrals throughout England and France, in particular the green-black Purbeck 'marble' mined here for the dark columns you may notice in Norman and early English cathedrals.

From the quarries and mines the stone was lowered into barges with derricks called 'whims' and taken to Swanage, and you may be able to trace some of the anchor points for the derricks.

With the tourist industry now bringing wealth once again to Britain's historical cities and monuments, the local quarries just inland are thriving and proudly continue a tradition of nearly 2,000 years.

The Tythe Barn Museum in Swanage has a display about local quarrying. If you follow the paths between Swanage and Worth Matravers, you will see the quarrymen at work extracting and dressing the stone.

Winspit quarries were last worked during the period of the Second World War.

Clay for the Staffordshire potteries

Clay is still extracted from traditional mines in Purbeck which in some cases are extremely deep. We know that, in 1820, 20,000 tons of clay a year were being shipped to Liverpool, and that one-third of the pottery made in England by the middle of the 19th century was made from Poole clay.

The clay came from the southern shores of Poole Harbour, and still does, and in the 19th century it was taken to quays on the headlands, tipped into 50-ton barges and transferred at Poole into sea-going ships. It has also been used locally for many centuries, and manufacture still goes on at Poole Pottery.

Gas lights for Paris

In the bands of shale at Kimmeridge there is a two-foot (60-centimetre) thick layer of the bituminous shale known as 'black stone' or 'Kimmeridge coal'. At various times it has been used as a fuel for industry. In the 17th century it was quarried to fuel an alum works and the alum was used for dyeing, printing and tanning.

Later a glass works was built at the Bay and this was excavated some years ago. You will find details of this in the Dorset Trust for Nature Conservation's Information Centre **71**.

During the 19th century an attempt was even made to supply the gasworks of Paris with Kimmeridge shale for Parisian street lighting. The contract fell through, however. One wonders whether the penetrating sulphurous smell deterred the Parisians. Local people used it to heat their houses right up until the 19th century.

The Romans used the shale to make ornaments, armlets and rings. Decorative chair legs made from the shale are in the County Museum at Dorchester and there is evidence that Iron Age people boiled sea water, using the shale as fuel, in order to manufacture salt. The salt-boiling works probably lie deep beneath the mounds of shale beside the cliff at Clavel Tower.

Oil for the 21st century

The search for oil has covered the whole of the area through which the Coast Path passes. The first drillings were unsuccessful, but as techniques improved and drills could go deeper, so more oil has been discovered.

The well at Kimmeridge Bay **70** has been operating since the late 1950s with a small but steady output. Then, some 20 years later, Wytch Farm oilfield on the southern shores of Poole

Harbour was discovered. Engineers have been at work there since the late 1970s, and after 1980 crude oil was pumped out at a rate of up to 4,000 barrels per day and exported by train on part of the old Swanage Railway. Most of this oil has come from the 'Bridport reservoir', which is a relatively shallow deposit.

With the discovery of the Sherwood reservoir, at a much deeper level, there has been an increase in daily production to 100,000 barrels per day.

This makes the islands and southern shores of Poole Harbour the largest on-shore oilfield in Europe. Production is planned to last for 20 years. Liquid gas is exported by rail, and oil goes by pipeline to the Solent.

The installations have been carefully sited to cause the minimum disturbance to wildlife, and carefully hidden so that it is difficult to see them at all. In recognition of this the project has won a Civic Trust award, the Queen's Award for Environmental Achievement, and many others.

Oil has been extracted from Kimmeridge Bay since the late 1950s.

The façade of Swanage Town Hall was once part of the Mercer's Hall in London

154

and was brought back as ballast.

PART THREE

USEFUL
INFORMATION

Transport

Rail

There are regular and frequent services to Exeter from all parts of Britain via London Waterloo, London Paddington, Bristol or Westbury. Change at Exeter St David's. From there to Exmouth there are half-hourly services Monday to Saturday, rather less frequently on Sundays in the winter.

The last stretch is usually in small diesel railcars from which you get fine views of the Exe Estuary. If you are not in too much of a hurry, it is well worth stopping at Topsham and Lympstone. For details see Crossing the Exe, page 22.

There are hourly services from London Waterloo to Poole and Weymouth, and daily through services avoiding London to all other parts of the country.

Booking is not required for any of these services. For time-table enquiries see 'British Rail' in your local phone book, or your local station.

For European visitors, international services from Brussels for Northern Europe and Paris from Southern Europe via the Channel Tunnel arrive at London Waterloo, and take three hours from city centre to city centre. Change platforms at Waterloo for direct express services to Exeter, Weymouth, Bournemouth or Poole for access to the beginning, middle or end of this section of the path. Apex (pay in advance) fares are generally cheaper than air, but more than bus/coach travel. For timetable and fare enquiries telephone (0345) 484950 (24-hour service).

Buses

There are normally daily express services by coach from all parts of the country to Exeter, Sidmouth, Seaton, Lyme, Weymouth and Poole. Tickets for these services should be bought in advance from travel agents or offices of the company concerned. For phone enquiries see 'National Express' in your local phone book.

There are services in the Exmouth–Lyme Regis sector, with buses using the main road which is never far from the coast, and regular stops at all the coastal towns along the route.

Coastal villages off the A35 in West Dorset, however, have only very intermittent services, or none at all; the same applies to Lulworth and Kimmeridge.

Worth Matravers, Langton, Swanage and Studland have good regular services with frequent connections to Wareham and Poole, with stops close to the railway stations.

For enquiries contact the following:

Wilts and Dorset Bus Company Ltd, Arndale Centre, Poole. Tel. Poole (01202) 678291.

Swanage Bus Station. Tel. Swanage (01929) 422528.

Devon General Bus Station. Tel. Exeter (01392) 427711.

Southern National, 18 South Street, Bridport. Tel. Bridport (01308) 422080; The Esplanade, Weymouth. Tel. Weymouth (01305) 783645; 39 St James's Street, Taunton. Tel. Taunton (01823) 272033. There may be special 'Explorer' tickets available from this firm, which are good value and useful when walking in the area.

Ferries

The Starcross Ferry runs an hourly service, seven days a week, from May to October. It leaves Starcross from 10 a.m. to 4 p.m. on the hour daily with an additional last ferry at 5 p.m. May to October, 5.45 p.m. in July and August. It leaves Exmouth for Starcross from 10.30 a.m. to 4.30 p.m. on the half hour, with an additional last ferry at 5.30 p.m. in May to October, 6.15 p.m. in July and August. Access to the ferry is through Starcross Station.

The Studland Chain Ferry operates a frequent service every day from early morning to late evening, with a brief break in late autumn for maintenance.

Contact the following for further information:

Exe Water Taxi Service operates from 8 a.m.–6 p.m. from April to the end of October, on request in person from the Exmouth side, or by hailing from the Dawlish Warren side, or by phoning the night before on (01392) 873409.

The Starcross Ferry (Starcross to Exmouth), Starcross Pier and Ferry Co., 26 Marine Parade, Dawlish. Tel. Dawlish (01626) 862452.

Bournemouth–Swanage Motor Road and Ferry Co., Floating Bridge, Sandbanks, Poole, Dorset. Tel. (01929) 450203.

Accommodation contacts

All the local tourist information centres can find you accommodation, including booking ahead bed and breakfast accommodation along your route. They try to make reservations for the time you ask, but if you leave this until the last minute during the school holiday periods you may have to go some distance inland. The centres are also well stocked with information about places to visit nearby, and in addition to free leaflets they have pamphlets and guides for sale. The staff can also suggest places to visit for a day out and direct you to Heritage Coast guided walks.

The following information centres are affiliated to the West Country Tourist Board, 60 St David's Hill, Exeter, Devon, EX4 4SY. Tel. Exeter (01392) 76351:

The Tourist Information Centre, Alexandra Terrace, Exmouth, Devon, EX8 1NZ. Tel. Exmouth (01395) 222299.

The Tourist Information Centre, Fore Street, Budleigh Salterton, Exeter, Devon, EX9 6NG. Tel. Budleigh Salterton (01395) 445275.

The Tourist Information Centre, The Esplanade, Ham Lane, Sidmouth, Exeter, Devon, EX10 8XR. Tel. Sidmouth (01395) 516441.

The Tourist Information Centre, Underfleet, Seaton, Devon, EX12 2TB. Tel. Seaton (01297) 21660.

The Tourist Information Centre, Guildhall Cottage, Church Street, Lyme Regis, Dorset, DT7 3BS. Tel. Lyme Regis (01297) 442138.

The Tourist Information Centre, 32 South Street, Bridport, Dorset, DT6 3NQ. Tel. Bridport (01308) 424901.

The Tourist Information Centre, The King's Statue, The Esplanade, Weymouth, Dorset, DT4 8ED. Tel. Weymouth (01305) 765221.

The boundary of the Southern Tourist Board is at Weymouth and its address is: 40 Chamberlayne Road, Eastleigh, Hampshire, SO50 5JH. Tel. Eastleigh (01703) 620006.

The only centre in this area which the Coast Path user will pass directly is at Swanage and the address is: Tourist Information Centre, Shore Road, Swanage, Dorset, BH19 1LB. Tel. Swanage (01929) 422885.

For camping see Ordnance Survey maps in this guide or ask

at the tourist information centres above. There is a camping barn at Little Catherston Farm, Charmouth, which provides inexpensive shelter for Coast Path walkers. Phone Charmouth (01297) 560550 for details.

The Rambler's Association yearbook and the South West Way Association guidebook, both published annually, list bed and breakfast places (see below and page 164 for addresses and phone numbers).

Other contacts

The Youth Hostels Association, Trevelyan House, 8 St Stephens Hill, St Albans, Herts, AL1 2DY. Tel. St Albans (01727) 855215.

The Ramblers' Association, 1–5 Wandsworth Road, London, SW8 2XX. Tel. London (0171) 582 6878. (Yearbook has many bed and breakfast addresses; available free to members; available to non-members from bookshops at $4.99 or direct from the R.A. (add $1.00 p. & p.).

The Association of Lightweight Campers, c/o The Camping and Caravanning Club, Greenfields House, Westwood Way, Coventry, CV4 8JH Tel. (01203) 694995.

The ruined Norman fortress of Corfe Castle.

Local organisations

You may like to join, or make a contribution or donation to, one of the local organisations which helps to look after the coast.

Coastal conservation and management is expensive these days, so even if you are already a member of the organisation concerned please put some money in the box if you have enjoyed the magnificent scenery which they are helping to protect. When added together these small donations all help the cause.

Devon Wildlife Trust, 35–37 St. Davids Hill, Exeter, Devon, EX4 4DA. Tel. Exeter (01392) 279244.

Dorset Wildlife Trust, Brooklands Farm, Forston, Dorchester, DT2 7AA. Tel. Dorchester (01305) 264620.

Dorset Natural History and Archaeological Society, Dorset County Museum, High West Street, Dorchester, DT1 1XA. Tel. Dor-chester (01305) 262735.

The South West Way Association, Membership Secretary, 25, Clobells, South Brent, Devon, TG10 9JW. Tel/Fax: 01364 73859. The South West Way Association exists to help those who enjoy walking this path. For advice about the Coast Path, phone Eric Wallis on (01752) 896237.

Other useful addresses

National Trust, Wessex Regional Office, Eastleigh Court, Bishopstrow, Warminster, Wilts, BA12 9HW. Tel. Warminster (01985) 843600.

National Trust, Devon Regional Office, Killerton House, Broadclyst, Exeter, EX5 3LE. Tel. Exeter (01392) 881691.

Royal Society for the Protection of Birds, The Lodge, Sandy, Beds, SG19 2DL. Tel. Sandy (01767) 680551.

English Nature, Roughmoor, Bishop's Hull, Taunton, Somerset, TA1 5AA. Tel. Taunton (01823) 283211.

Countryside Commission, South West Regional Office, Bridge House, Sion Place, Clifton Down, Bristol, BS8 4AS. Tel. Bristol (0117) 9739966.

Countryside Commission (Headquarters), John Dower House, Crescent Place, Cheltenham, Glos, GL50 3RA. Tel. Cheltenham (01242) 521381.

Ordnance Survey, Romsey Road, Maybush, Southampton, SO16 4GU. Tel. Southampton (01703) 792000.

South West Coast Path Team, c/o Devon County Council, County Hall, Exeter, EX2 4QW. Tel. (01392) 383560.

Guided walks

Many guided walks are now conducted along the route of the path. They are led by local experts and can add a completely new dimension to a holiday on this coast. The normal duration is a couple of hours.

Between Easter and October copies of the programmes may be obtained from tourist information centres, Heritage Coast information centres, public libraries and museums. Some are organised privately and others by local civic and naturalists' societies, often in conjunction with the Dorset and East Devon Heritage Coasts.

Nearby places of interest

Exeter – cathedral, museum, Georgian houses.

East Budleigh – Raleigh's birthplace, interesting village and church with many Raleigh reminders.

Otterton Mill – working mill open to the public, with corn grinding demonstrations, stone-ground flour and home-made bread for sale, tea rooms.

Bicton Gardens – formal gardens of an early 18th century stately home which is now an agricultural college.

Sidmouth – Regency and Victorian buildings of style and elegance, and museum.

Bovey House – now a hotel and restaurant, 1 mile (1.5 km) north of Beer, built in 1592 with Jacobean carvings in hall and dining room and a restoration ceiling in the King Charles Room.

Seaton – Axe Valley Heritage Museum above Town Hall.

Forde Abbey – beautiful house and gardens based on medieval abbey.

Upwey – the Wishing Well, ancient monument.

Dorchester – Old Crown Court where the Tolpuddle Martyrs were tried, Roman town house and wall, the walks which surround the town on the line of the Roman ramparts, Roman amphitheatre, medieval churches, County Museum with displays on prehistory, Roman mosaics, and Thomas Hardy's study. Max Gate, Hardy's house, is open. Ask local T.I.C. or see N.T. handbook for times.

Wolfeton House – within walking or cycling distance just north of Dorchester. Spanish Armada exhibits. Small but very intriguing country manor house open May–Sept, Tues, Fri and Sun 2 p.m. to 6 p.m., and in August daily except Sat.

Wareham – Saxon ramparts complete, two medieval churches, one Saxon or early Norman, and one with very early Christian inscriptions. Quay on River Frome and some fine old town houses.

Corfe Castle (NT) – Purbeck stone village and massive Norman fortress which played an important role in many episodes of English history.

Studland – important heathland nature reserves managed by Nature Conservancy Council. Solid Norman village church.

Bibliography

Austen, Jane, *Persuasion* (Chatto & Windus, and Penguin, 1970).

Barns, Norman, *The East Devon Way: A walkers inland route from the Exe to the Lym.* (E. Devon District Council, 1993).

Betty, J. H., *The Landscape of Wessex* (Moonraker Press, 1986, revised edition 1996).

Blatchford, Barbara, *The Long Distance Walker's Handbook* (A. & C. Black, 1986).

Bond, Lilian, *Tyneham, A Lost Heritage* (Dovecote Press, 1984).

Burnett, David, *Dorset Shipwrecks* (Dovecote Press, 1982).

Butler, Richard (ed.), *A View from the Cliffs* (Devon Books). A guide to the East Devon Heritage Coast.

Coxe, A. Hippisley, *Smuggling in the West Country* (Tabb House, 1984).

Cullingford, Cecil, *A History of Dorset* (Phillimore & Co., 1980).

Dorset, Landranger Guidebook (OS and Jarrold, 1987).

Draper, Jo, *Dorset: The Complete Guide* (Dovecote Press, 1986, revised edition 1996).

Durrance, E. and Laming, D., *The Geology of Devon* (University of Exeter Press, 1982).

Falkner, J. M., *Moonfleet* (Penguin, 1979).

Fowles, John, *A Short History of Lyme Regis* (Dovecote Press, 1982).

——*The French Lieutenant's Woman* (Jonathan Cape, 1969 and Panther, 1971).

——and Draper, Jo, *Thomas Hardy's England* (Jonathan Cape, 1984).

Hardy, Thomas, *The Trumpet Major* and other novels.

Heritage Coast leaflet packs, on sale at tourist information centres and local outlets: round walks (green cover); Purbeck (yellow); wildlife (blue); West Dorset (blue).

Kay-Robinson, Denys, *The Landscape of Thomas Hardy* (Webb & Bower, 1984).

The National Trust Coast of Devon (Devon Books).

Ordnance Survey Leisure Guides, *Devon* with *Exmoor*, and *Wessex* (OS and AA, 1988).

Pitfield, F.P., *Purbeck Parish Churches* (Dorset Publishing Co., 1981).

Royal Commission for Historical Monuments, *Dorset* (8 vols, HMSO, 1952 and 1970).

Sanctuary, A., *Rope, Twine and Net Making* (Shire Publications, 1980).

Wallington, Mark, *500 Mile Walkies* (Hutchinson/Arrow, 1986).

Welfare, Humphrey, *Wessex*. National Trust Histories (NT/Collins Willow, 1984).

Wilkinson, Gerald, *Woodland Walks in South West England* (OS and Webb & Bower, 1986).

The Dorset Countyside Book, an annual publication with over 350 walks and events in Dorset is available from Dorset tourist information centres listed above or from County Hall, Dorchester DT1 1BR ($1.95 + 57p p. & p.)

Ordnance Survey Maps covering the South West Coast Path (Exmouth to Poole)

Landranger Maps: 192, 193, 194, 195.
Explorer Maps
    29 Lyme Regis & Bridport
    30 Exmouth & Sidmouth
Outdoor Leisure Map: Map 15, Purbeck and South Dorset covers the rest of the area at 1:25,000.
Motoring Maps: Reach the South West Coast Path area using Routemaster Maps 8, 'South West England and South Wales' and 9, 'South East England'.